St. Mary's High School

Ice Hockey

ANNE WALLACE SHARP

LUCENT BOOKS
A part of Gale, Cengage Learning

Detroit • New York • San Francisco • New Haven, Conn • Waterville, Maine • London

LIBRARY OF CONGRESS CATALOGING-IN-PUBLICATION DATA

Sharp, Anne Wallace.
   Ice hockey / by Anne Wallace Sharp.
      p. cm. — (The science behind sports)
   Includes bibliographical references and index.
   ISBN 978-1-4205-0281-7 (hardcover)
 1. Hockey—Juvenile literature. 2. Sports sciences—Juvenile literature. I. Title.
   GV847.25.S43 2010
   796.962—dc22
                                                                    2010025670

Lucent Books
27500 Drake Rd
Farmington Hills MI 48331

ISBN-13: 978-1-4205-0281-7
ISBN-10: 1-4205-0281-6

Printed in the United States of America
1 2 3 4 5 6 7 14 13 12 11 10

Printed by Bang Printing, Brainerd, MN, 1st Ptg., 10/2010

TABLE OF CONTENTS

FOREWORD

On March 21, 1970, Slovenian ski jumper Vinko Bogataj took a terrible fall while competing at the Ski-flying World Championships in Oberstdorf, West Germany. Bogataj's pinwheeling crash was caught on tape by an ABC *Wide World of Sports* film crew and eventually became synonymous with "the agony of defeat" in competitive sporting. While many viewers were transfixed by the severity of Bogataj's accident, most were not aware of the biomechanical and environmental elements behind the skier's fall—heavy snow and wind conditions that made the ramp too fast and Bogataj's inability to maintain his center of gravity and slow himself down. Bogataj's accident illustrates that, no matter how mentally and physically prepared an athlete may be, scientific principles—such as momentum, gravity, friction, and aerodynamics—always have an impact on performance.

Lucent Book's Science Behind Sports series explores these and many more scientific principles behind some of the most popular team and individual sports, including baseball, hockey, gymnastics, wrestling, swimming, and skiing. Each volume in the series focuses on one sport or group of related sports. The volumes open with a brief look at the featured sport's origins, history and changes, then move on to cover the biomechanics and physiology of playing, related health and medical concerns, and the causes and treatment of sports-related injuries.

In addition to learning about the arc behind a curve ball, the impact of centripetal force on a figure skater, or how water buoyancy helps swimmers, Science Behind Sports readers will also learn how exercise, training, warming up, and diet and nutrition directly relate to peak performance and enjoyment of the sport. Volumes may also cover why certain sports are popular, how sports function in the business world, and which hot sporting issues—sports doping and cheating, for example—are in the news.

Basic physical science concepts, such as acceleration, kinetics, torque, and velocity, are explained in an engaging and accessible manner. The full-color text is augmented by fact boxes, sidebars, photos, and detailed diagrams, charts and graphs. In addition, a subject-specific glossary, bibliography and index provide further tools for researching the sports and concepts discussed throughout Science Behind Sports.

CHAPTER 1

A Lightning Fast Game: The Story of Ice Hockey

Ice hockey is a game of lightning-fast action that is both thrilling to watch and to play. With players skating as fast as 30 miles per hour (48kmh) and the puck traveling at speeds up to 100 miles per hour (161kmh), hockey is also the fastest professional contact sport played today.

The game of ice hockey has been described by the Society for International Hockey Research as "a game played on the ice rink in which opposing teams of skaters, using curved sticks, try to drive a small disc, ball, or puck into or through the opposition's goal."[1] Players must be proficient in skating, shooting, passing, checking or blocking other players, and stopping the puck. They must also have a high level of endurance and be in peak physical condition to play one of the most demanding games in sports.

The game of ice hockey has been around for hundreds of years. Historians believe that the modern game of ice hockey derives from various ball-and-stick games played throughout the world by indigenous people. The ancient Egyptians and the Mayans of Central America, for instance, both played such games on courts made specifically for the sport. It is

believed that these games were the forerunners of many of today's sports.

In 1997, during an excavation for a golf course in Colorado, builders found further proof of the early origins of ball-and-stick games. Journalist Alisha Jeter describes a sculpture that was uncovered: "The piece depicts five life-size Cheyenne Indians engaged in the ancient game of shinny in which a ball is hit on a field."[2] Golf, field hockey, lacrosse, and ice hockey all have their origins in these early sports contests.

These ball-and-stick games have been played all over the world, and in many cases, are still being played today. The early Scots, for instance, called their game shinny, or shinty, a popular game played using any kind of stick the players could find. The game could be played anywhere there was a large enough field. Shinny remains a popular sport today and can be played either on ice or on any surface large enough for the players to compete.

The Scottish game shinty and other early ball-and-stick games helped develop the modern game of ice hockey.

Early Forms of Hockey

Archaeological findings suggest that groups of native people in the northern areas of the world were playing a ball-and-stick game on the ice many centuries ago. These games were played using bent sticks and a painted or curved wooden ball. The object was to hit the ball through the opposing team's goal. Ten men played on each team. The Micmac tribe of eastern Canada, for instance, called their game *tooadijik*. Other names for the game were used by indigenous people in other lands.

The English and Russians played a similar game called bandy as early as the tenth and eleventh centuries. This game originated as a form of field hockey played on ice. It was especially popular in Russia because of the long winters there. Bandy was played using a stick and ball. Two teams of eleven players competed to get the ball into the other team's goal. Today bandy is still a very popular sport, and it is played in the United States and throughout the world.

A game called hurley was played in Great Britain, Ireland, and France as far back as the sixteenth century. It was played in the winter, when the fields were frozen. Players used a ball that was hit with some kind of wooden club. Players strapped blades made of wood or bone onto their shoes to help propel them across the freezing tundra. By the seventeenth century, almost every European country with a cold climate played some form of the game.

By the middle of the nineteenth century, the Dutch developed a primitive but more practical form of ice skates by strapping metal blades onto their shoes. The blades allowed the skaters to perform with more balance and speed. They gave the players better traction on the ice, and the blades were also less likely to come loose and cause falls. Ice hockey increased in popularity as a result of the new skates.

The word *hockey*, however, did not come into existence until the end of the nineteenth century. There are several theories about the origin of the term. Some historians believe it comes from the French word *hocquet*, a word

POWER PLAY

Ice hockey was the first sport to place numbers on the backs of players' jerseys.

describing the shape of a shepherd's crook, since a hockey stick resembles the crook. Other historians claim that the game is named after a colonel who was stationed in Nova Scotia, Canada. Colonel Hockey is reputed to have ordered his troops to play hurley on the ice during the winter months.

Hockey Arrives in North America

Whatever the origin of the name, ice hockey was brought to Canada from Great Britain and other European countries during the 1800s. Hockey soon became the country's official national winter sport. While the Canadians did not invent the game of hockey, they are credited with refining it into the game that is played today.

Historical records indicate that the first semiofficial game occurred in Kingston, Ontario, in the 1850s between Canadian soldiers stationed there. Three different Canadian cities later claimed the credit for introducing ice hockey to North America: Halifax, Kingston, and Montreal. The first officially sanctioned hockey game, however, played with a flat circular piece of wood and complete with written rules and regulations, was played in 1875 at McGill University in Montreal. According to Gary Abraham, a sports medicine specialist in youth hockey, "it was organized by James Creighton, a Halifax engineer whom many call the father of organized ice hockey."[3] Creighton, a hockey player himself for the Rideau Rebels, an Ottawa hockey club, was also the first person to stage an indoor hockey game. For the indoor game a square piece of rubber called a puck replaced the ball that had been used for centuries.

In 1890 the Ontario Hockey Association was formed; it was the first organization created to administer the increasingly popular game of ice hockey. During the late nineteenth century, many Canadian towns and cities had hockey teams. These teams played in unorganized leagues, and their games were fiercely competitive. Many cities had more than one team. The players on these teams were not paid by anyone to play.

Many of the rules used in these early games became the basis for the rules that are used today in modern hockey.

However, the game that was played in the late nineteenth century barely resembles the modern one. There were nine players on each team, and players did not wear any protective equipment. In addition, players were not allowed to make any forward passes. Spectators stood on the edge of the ice with no protection from flying pucks.

One thing that has not changed, however, is the size of hockey ice rinks. Rink dimensions were first established by the ice surface at Montreal's Victoria Skating Rink, which was 200 feet (61m) by 85 feet (26m).

U.S. Ice Hockey

Ice hockey first appeared in the United States in the late nineteenth century. Initially only those living in the Northeast and Upper Midwest, where the climate was amenable to the creation of frozen ponds and lakes, were interested in the game. As late as 1895, many American teams, as well as Canadian ones, were still using a ball instead of a puck, because of the availability of balls and the higher cost of pucks. More formalized hockey began with a game between teams from Yale University and Johns Hopkins University in 1893.

The first professional ice hockey league was based in Houghton, Michigan, and from there grew into Canada and many other countries. While still largely a game played by amateurs and college students, hockey took a more professional turn in 1904 when the first professional hockey league, the International Hockey League was formed. Teams from both the United States and Canada belonged to the league. After the 1906–07 season, the league ended. Many teams disbanded as players wanted to play closer to home and in front of home crowds. Also there were more professional opportunities in Canada, which drew back players from the IHL. These professional Canadian teams, located mainly in Ontario and Quebec, formed the National Hockey Association, which ran from 1910–17.

In 1917 the National Hockey Association dissolved as some team executives pealed off to form the National Hockey League. Initially, only Canadian teams belonged to this professional league and they played against the Pacific Coast Hockey Association for the championship title. In 1924, however, the Boston Bruins of Massachusetts were invited to join and other United States teams soon followed. The league then expanded quickly and after 1926 the championship was determined within the league.

Olympic Ice Hockey

Hockey teams from many countries in Europe and North America compete every four years in the Olympic Games. Men's ice hockey became an Olympic event in 1920 (women's ice hockey first appeared at the 1998 Olympics). Seven teams entered that first competition: Canada, the United States, Switzerland, Belgium, France, Sweden, and Czechoslovakia. Canada won in 1920 and in five of the next six competitions, while the Russian team dominated the competition in the 1960s and 1970s.

One of the most startling victories in Olympic ice hockey history came in 1980 when a team of amateur players from the United States captured the gold medal in a stunning upset of the heavily favored Russian and Finnish teams. Called the Miracle on Ice, the game between the United States and the Soviet Union heightened interest in hockey in the United States. Sports historians consider the U.S. victory one of the greatest upsets in sports history.

The Olympic hockey game between the United States and the Soviet Union, nicknamed the Miracle on Ice, raised U.S. interest in ice hockey.

For seventy-seven years only amateurs could compete in Olympic ice hockey. Starting in 1998, National Hockey League players (professional athletes) were allowed to participate in the Olympics.

The National Hockey League

Professional ice hockey started slowly and gradually began to attract more and more interest and money. During the early years of the National Hockey League, the game was quite different than it is today. In the beginning, players could not pass the puck forward, goalies could not drop to the ice and smother the puck, and the

Hockey player Bep Guidolin played for the Boston Bruins, one of so-called "original six" teams that made up the NHL in 1942.

rules were constantly changing. Hockey historian Douglas Hunter explains, "[Hockey's] most fundamental rules were revised ceaselessly, even decades into its existence as a popular professional sport. Baseball as played in the 1920s was much the same as it is today, but a hockey fan transported back into a rinkside seat before the Depression [in the 1930s] would find the game decidedly odd."[4] Gradually, however, many of the rules changed, and the more modern game of hockey emerged.

TODAY'S NATIONAL HOCKEY LEAGUE

Vancouver Canucks (NW)
Edmonton Oilers (NW)
Calgary Flames (NW)
CANADA
Montreal Canadiens (NE)
Ottawa Senators (NE)
Minnesota Wild (NW)
Toronto Maple Leafs (NE)
Buffalo Sabres (NE)
Boston Bruins (NE)
New York Rangers (A)
Detroit Red Wings (C)
Philadelphia Flyers (A)
New York Islanders (A)
San Jose Sharks (P)
Phoenix Coyotes (P)
Chicago Blackhawks (C)
Pittsburgh Penguins (A)
New Jersey Devils (A)
Colorado Avalanche (NW)
Columbus Blue Jackets (C)
St Louis Blues (C)
Washington [D.C.] Capitals (S)
Los Angeles Kings (P)
Carolina Hurricanes (S)
Nashville Predators (C)
Anaheim Ducks (P)
Atlanta Thrashers (S)
Dallas Stars (P)
Tampa Bay Lightning (S)
Florida Panthers (S)

Eastern Conference
(A) Atlantic
(NE) Northeast
(S) Southeast

Western Conference
(C) Central
(NW) Northwest
(P) Pacific

Today, the National Hockey League is made up of 30 teams from both Canada and the United States. They are evenly divided into two conferences—Eastern and Western—with each conference consisting of three divisions.

A Return to the Outdoors

Professional ice hockey returned to its outdoor roots on January 1, 2008, when the Pittsburgh Penguins played the Buffalo Sabres on an ice-covered field at the home of the Buffalo Bills football team. Over seventy-one thousand fans endured the freezing cold to see the game in person, while the television broadcast drew one of the largest audiences ever for an ice hockey game.

Hockey's golden age began in 1942 and lasted for twenty-five years. During that time, the National Hockey League had only six teams: the Boston Bruins, the Chicago Blackhawks, the New York Rangers, the Detroit Red Wings, the Montreal Canadiens, and the Toronto Maple Leafs. This period was "golden" because of the immense popularity of the game and the fierce rivalry that existed between the original six teams.

It was during this time that the season was expanded to seventy games. The season used to have twenty-four games during the early part of the twentieth century, and forty-eight games prior to World War II.

The composition of professional hockey teams also changed during this period. In the early years of professional hockey, the teams were made up of only Canadian and American players. That changed in the 1990s when players from all over the world were recruited to play in North America. The fall of the Berlin wall and the collapse of the former Soviet Union made it possible for players from Communist countries to play for the first time in North America. The first was Sergei Priakin from Russia in 1989. He was soon joined by hundreds of players from Russia, Czechoslovakia, Sweden, Finland, and elsewhere.

Today the National Hockey League has thirty teams from Canada and the United States. Six teams were added to the original six in 1967, with additional expansions in 1981 and 1993. There are two conferences, the Eastern and the Western, each of which is composed of three divisions. At the end of the season, the Eastern Conference champion plays the Western Conference champion in a best of seven series to determine the champion, or Stanley Cup winner. (In a best of seven series a team must win four out of seven games to win.) The Stanley Cup, an immense trophy, has been awarded to ice hockey's best team since the late nineteenth century.

Ice hockey has also become a popular sport on television. In 1952 the Canadian Broadcasting Company (CBC) began transmitting television signals in Canada, first from Montreal and then Toronto. The first televised game was broadcast on November 1, 1952, from Toronto, allowing avid hockey fans in Canada to watch their favorite sport without being at the arena. The CBC continues today to broadcast "Hockey Night in Canada" every Saturday to viewers in Canada and the United States.

Changes in the Game

Since the inception of the game of ice hockey, there have been many changes in the game. In the early years, each hockey team was made up of nine players on the ice, today's game features only six players—a goalie, two defensemen, two wings, and a center. These players, with the exception of the goalie, are replaced throughout the game in a continuous process, allowing no one player to average more than a minute or so of ice time at any given point. Each team is allotted twenty players and two goalies. Some players will average more ice time per game than others, depending on their level of skill.

A face-off is used to begin each hockey game. A player from one team faces a player from the other team at center ice; the referee then drops the puck and the play begins by the team who gains possession of the puck. The professional game is divided into three, twenty-minute periods, with a rest interval of twenty minutes between periods. In a game that ends in a tie score, the victor will be determined during a five-minute sudden-death overtime. This means that the first team that scores wins. If no winner is determined in overtime, the teams will determine the victor through a process called a shoot-out. During a shoot-out, three players from each team try individually to shoot a puck into the goal, guarded by the goalie. The team who scores the most times wins the game. If no winner is determined after the original three players, the shoot-out continues with additional players until one team wins the game.

Standings (rankings of first, second, third, etc. in a division) in the National Hockey League are based on a point system in

A face-off at center ice is used to begin play in a hockey game.

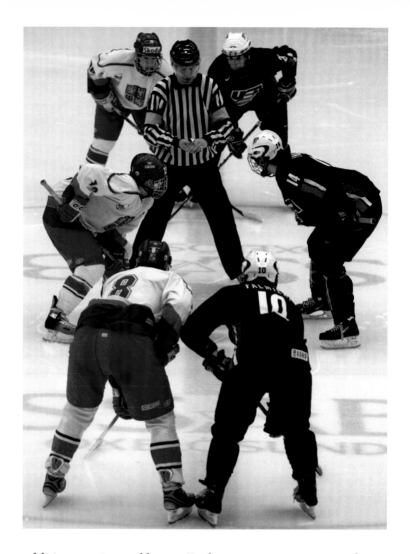

addition to wins and losses. Each team earns two points for an outright win in regulation time (60 minutes); one point for a tie and an additional point for winning during overtime or a shoot-out. No more than two points are added per game. At the end of the season, the teams with the highest point counts are division champions. Teams are eliminated in a series of playoff games until there is an Eastern Conference champion and a Western Conference champion. These two teams play for the Stanley Cup.

Modern ice hockey also makes use of a series of penalties that can send the offending player off the ice, usually to a penalty box, for anywhere from two to ten minutes. (If it is near the end of a period, players are sometimes sent to the locker room instead of the penalty box.) The offending player's team is then required to play one man short for the duration of the penalty which allows the other team an opportunity to score with a man advantage; this is called a power play. Most penalties are categorized as "minor" penalties and last two minutes. Minor penalties are called for tripping, roughing (fighting) that does not cause bleeding, high-sticking (touching the opponent's upper body with the stick), holding, interference, hooking (using the stick to slow an opponent), delay of game, and too many men on the ice.

Other Forms of Hockey

There are many forms of hockey played today. Underwater hockey, for instance, is played in a swimming pool. A puck, known as a "squib" in Great Britain, has a lead core interior weighing 3 pounds (1.4kg). The added weight makes the puck heavy enough to sink in water, but light enough that it can be passed. It is covered with a Teflon, plastic, or rubber coating and painted bright orange or pink. Sticks are made of wood or thick plastic and measure about 12 inches (30cm) long.

Sledge hockey is another adaptation of the game. This sport was created in Norway in 1967 for athletes with severe lower body injuries. Players use a sled and play on a standard-size rink with six players. The sleds have skate blades for easy movement, while players use two sticks with ice picks on the bottom to push themselves around the rink and handle the puck. Competitors play in leagues and also in

Sledge hockey was created for athletes with severe lower body injuries.

the Winter Paralympics, an Olympic event that features over four hundred physically impaired athletes competing in a variety of sports. Radio broadcaster Howard Berkes describes one player: "United States goalie Manny Guerra played stand-up hockey before polio put him in a sled…. When he's on the ice, he wants to be seen as a hockey player, not a disabled athlete."

Howard Berkes, "Sledge Hockey," *All Things Considered,* National Public Radio, March 8, 2002.

Major penalties of five minutes are given for more serious offenses. These involve injury to another player as well as fighting. In some instances, if a serious infraction or injury occurs, the offending player is given a game misconduct penalty, is ejected from the game, and not allowed to return to the ice. Depending on the league, two to four ice officials are responsible for calling penalties and for enforcing the rules. Four officials (two referees and two linesmen) are used in most professional hockey games.

Women's Hockey

Hockey is not just a game for men; it is also played by an ever-increasing number of women. From 2000 to 2010 ice hockey became one of the fastest growing women's sports in the world.

Although many girls skated in the 1800s, hockey was considered unladylike and few women dared to challenge the strict cultural norms. In the late 1880s, however, Lord Frederick Stanley of Preston, the governor general of Canada, and his hockey-loving family gave women the chance to play the game in public. He built a rink at the Government House in Ottawa where he, his wife, their eight sons, and two daughters played. By 1889, women in Great Britain were also taking to the ice in large numbers. They formed teams and competed in games wearing layers of petticoats under ankle-length skirts. Their long-sleeved blouses were usually buttoned to the chin.

Women's teams in Canada and the United States began competing for the first time in 1916. Despite the number of women playing, the game remained largely unknown to the general public. *New York Times* reporter Andrea Kannapell writes, "For most of [the twentieth] century, [women's hockey] was in retreat, hiding out at prep schools and Ivy League colleges."[5] Many girls and women who wanted to play hockey, in fact, were forced to play on boy's and men's teams.

Women eventually wanted more control over the hockey leagues in which they played and in 1922 formed the Ladies Ontario Hockey Association. For the first time, women players were able to make decisions about their own game.

The major difference in the men's and women's game is that no body checking (stopping an opponent through the use of physical contact) is allowed in women's hockey. Girls are no longer forced to play on boy's teams; in fact, today girls are discouraged from playing boys' hockey. This is due to the physical difference between the two sexes.

Girls develop differently than boys; they gain more body fat, whereas boys add muscle. Before puberty, boys and girls often compete on the same teams, but as boys grow, their build and size give them an advantage.

Interest in women's hockey increased in the late twentieth century especially after the game was added to the 1998 Olympic Games. Abraham explains, "A lot of the increased growth in girls' hockey is due to the Women's World Championship, first held in 1990. But the greatest boost was the 1998 Winter Olympic Games in Nagano, Japan, where women's hockey finally became an Olympic medal sport."[6] The United States won the gold medal at that first Olympic event.

The number of females playing ice hockey has skyrocketed in just the last two decades. In 1990, for example, there were 149 United States girls' and women's teams. Today nearly sixty thousand girls and women play ice hockey.

Women Players

Much of the increased popularity in women's hockey is due to the accomplishments of several girls and women. In 1955, for instance, eight-year-old Abby Hoffman made headlines when she signed up as "Ab Hoffman" for a local boy's hockey league. Her teammates did not know she was female; dressed in all the typical hockey gear, she looked like all the other players. Ab Hoffman made the All-Star Team and was named one of the best defensemen in the league. It was then that newspaper reporters discovered that Ab Hoffman was a girl. Her photograph and story appeared in papers throughout North America. She was allowed to continue playing on the boy's team until the end of the season, and she retired from hockey at the end of the year. She went on to have a great career in track and field. Hoffman is credited for the creation of many girls' leagues throughout North America. Today the Abby Hoffman Cup is given to the national champion of Canadian women's hockey.

The U.S. women's hockey team celebrates winning the gold medal at the 1998 Olympic Games in Japan. The establishment of women's ice hockey as an Olympic sport helped skyrocket the sport's popularity.

In 1992 Manon Rheaume made another kind of history when she became the first woman to sign a National Hockey League contract with the Tampa Bay Lightning, an all-male professional team. She played goalie in one exhibition game against the St. Louis Blues. General manager of the Lightning, Phil Esposito, had seen Rheaume play in a junior hockey

Lord Stanley and the Stanley Cup

Lord Frederick Stanley of Preston, governor general of Canada in the late nineteenth century, lent his name to one of the most enduring prizes in sports history. In 1893 he presented an award to the champion of the Amateur Hockey Association of Canada. That first Stanley Cup, the oldest trophy in professional sports, was awarded to the Winged Wheelmen of Montreal Amateur Athletic Association. At that time, the award was simply called the Dominion Challenge Trophy.

In the early days of competition for the Stanley Cup, any team from any town could compete for the cup. As the game became more professionally oriented, bigger towns became more prominent because of the high cost of paying the best hockey players. When the professional National Hockey League was created, the trophy was given to the winning team, beginning in 1947. Since that time, the Stanley Cup has been awarded each year as a symbol of hockey supremacy.

The original Stanley Cup was 7 inches (17.8cm) high. The modern version first appeared in 1958 in a five-band barrel shape that weighs 35 pounds (16kg) and stands 35 inches (89cm) high.

The Governor General of Canada, Lord Stanley of Preston, pictured left, presented the first Stanley Cup, pictured right, in 1893.

The Stanley Cup has served as a baptismal vessel and a bowl for dog food. It has been to the White House; it has been a guest on the late-night television show *The Late Show with David Letterman*; and it has visited the Kremlin in Russia. In 2007 the cup made its first trip to a war zone when it was taken to Afghanistan. The 1896 tradition of drinking champagne from the cup continues to this day.

tournament. He was impressed with her talent and, hoping to generate interest in ice hockey to the warm-weather climate and populace of Florida, he signed her. After her brief appearance for the Lightning, Rheaume went on to have a stellar career in the East Coast Hockey League, a men's minor league. She also played on Canada's team in the first women's hockey tournament in the Olympics; the team won the silver medal in 1998. Other women to play in men's professional hockey leagues across the globe include Erin Whitten, Kelly Dyer, Hayley Wickenheiser, and Kira Hurley.

One of the greatest women's hockey teams in history was the Preston Rivulettes of Canada. Formed by sisters Hilda and Nellie Ranscombe in 1930, the team went on to become a nearly unbeatable team. With Hilda playing right wing and Nellie playing goalie, the team amassed an amazing record of 348 wins and only 2 losses. From 1930 to 1939, the team won ten championship titles in Quebec and Ontario, as well as six national titles.

Youth Hockey

The popularity of men's and women's hockey has resulted in an ever-increasing interest in youth hockey. According to Abraham, "well over a million kids play hockey in North America. The game has become a large part of our culture."[7]

Youth hockey teams are organized by age. In general most children begin playing ice hockey around the age of five. As the players age, they are moved up to more advanced teams and compete with other teams in the same age group. Most youth teams have fifteen to seventeen players. Teams are usually supported by local businesses and parents pay a fee for their child to play. Teams compete in anywhere from eight to twelve games a year, along with various tournaments for each age level.

Most children wear so much protective gear that their weight is nearly doubled. Unlike in the professional leagues, all players are required to wear helmets and face guards similar to the mask worn by goalies. Coaches run highly structured practices, stressing the importance of skills and proper conditioning. The youth leagues all come under the watchful eye of youth hockey organizations in both Canada and the United States.

Today more than two thousand young hockey players from sixteen different countries gather once a year in Quebec City, Canada, to play in the World Championships. This tournament is an eleven-day event in which eleven and twelve year olds compete. Many great professional hockey players have started in the sport in youth leagues around the world.

Players can get further experience in colleges in both Canada and the United States. Competition is fierce throughout the collegiate ranks, especially in the United States. American teams, for instance, play a season-ending tournament called the Frozen Four.

Ice hockey continues to grow in popularity at all levels of competition. Much of this popularity can be traced to such superstars as Mario Lemieux and Wayne Gretzky, who dominated the National Hockey League for years in the 1980s and 1990s. Big rivalries between teams also engendered interest and has helped promote the sport. Today's heroes include superstar Alex Ovechkin, and past Olympians Cammi Granato and Manon Rheaume. As a result of the increased popularity of the sport, many teams sell out their season tickets each year, and the television audience is growing as well. Today ice hockey remains an exciting and action-packed game at all levels of play.

CHAPTER 2

Ice, Skates, and Collisions

Millions of people watch the thrilling sport of ice hockey. Spectators are fascinated by the high-speed intensity of the game. Yet, those same people seldom question the whys and hows of ice hockey. They love the indoor ice rinks but rarely wonder how the ice is made; they are amazed at the high speed skating but may never question the technology that makes skates work so effectively. Spectators are also thrilled with the powerful collisions that occur between players, perhaps never once wondering about the power and energy that such a collision creates.

What these millions of fans may not know is that the game they all love would not be possible without science. Several scientific principles, in fact, are at work each time a hockey player takes the ice; in particular, the concepts of speed, velocity, friction, momentum, motion, energy, and force. Science has also played a vital role in the creation of quality ice and ice skates.

Making Ice

Ice surfaces have improved dramatically since the early days of hockey, when players were forced to find their own ice. Any frozen pond or other body of water would do. These surfaces were often snow covered and bumpy, but they

In ice hockey, the first few layers of the ice surface are generally painted with a team's logo. Then, an additional eight to ten layers of ice are added.

served as rinks for the earliest hockey players. Because of the need for a surface of ice, hockey could only be played during the coldest winter months.

Historians are not sure who first invented artificial ice, but by the 1870s, hockey could be played indoors in many areas. By the early 1900s, covered ice surfaces or arenas were popping up all over North America. The technology used to make and maintain the indoor ice, however, was very expensive. Most games, therefore, were still played on natural outdoor ice until the 1940s and 1950s when a less costly method of freezing the surface was developed.

Today's game is played on specially made ice rinks in large indoor arenas. Before the first hockey game of the season, ice makers throughout the National Hockey League are busy at work preparing their arena's ice surface. Most arenas have an advanced refrigeration system that is capable of pumping large amounts of saltwater through a system of pipes into a large piece of concrete, known as the ice slab. Saltwater, or brine water, a calcium chloride solution, is used to cool the slab because it has a low freezing temperature and will keep circulating to keep the ice slab at a steady temperature. Freshwater, on the other hand, freezes quicker, and would stop the water from circulating.

Once the slab reaches a cold enough temperature, about 26°F (−3.3°C), layer after layer of water is applied to the slab to build up the proper density and thickness of the ice, usually 0.75-inch (1.9cm) thick. The proper ice thickness is crucial to the game of hockey. Journalist Melissa Russell-Ausley explains, "An ice surface that is too thick requires more energy to keep frozen and is prone to getting soft on the top. A surface that is too thin is also dangerous because skaters risk cutting straight through the ice."[8]

The first few layers of the ice surface, generally only about 0.03-inch (0.08cm) thick, are usually painted with the team's logo and certain advertisements that are part of today's ice hockey. An additional eight to ten layers of ice are added, bringing the total frozen water used to over 10,000 gallons (37,854L). The water is applied slowly, usually about 600 gallons (2,271L) at a time. Ice supervisor Don MacMillan of the Carolina Hurricanes professional ice hockey team says "The less water you put on the floor at one time, the better your ice will be."[9] Applying the water too quickly or in large quantities results in an uneven surface with many irregularities that would endanger the skaters. This ice stays in place from September to May, or even longer, if the team does well in the playoffs.

POWER PLAY

An ice surface in a Florida arena is at risk of more "melting" than one in a Canadian arena because the weather in Florida is so warm. Simply opening and closing the outside doors can change the temperature in Florida's buildings.

Quality of the Ice

The quality of the ice is very important for hockey players. The terms *fast ice* and *slow ice* are commonplace in hockey leagues around the world. According to scientists, "fast ice

The Zamboni—a mechanical ice resurfacer—is the primary method used to keep the ice solid and smooth.

is harder and colder with a smoother surface, while slow ice is warm and soft and may have rough surfaces."[10]

Ice maker Bruce Tharaldson, who works for the San Jose Sharks, explains, "Keeping the ice cold is one of the keys to maintaining fast ice."[11] The ideal temperature for the ice is 16°F (−8.9°C). Maintaining this temperature is more difficult in milder climates because of the outside air temperature.

To help keep the ice solid and "fast," the ice is treated after each hockey period. One of the primary tools used to treat the ice is the Zamboni machine, named after its inventor, Frank Zamboni. The Zamboni is a mechanical ice resurfacer that works by scraping the ice and collecting (and later discarding) any snow that has collected. The next step is cleaning the ice by putting down water which flushes the ice of any dirt or debris. The final step is putting down a thin layer of heated water that melts the top layer of ice.

The warm water also fills any cracks and holes in the ice made from the players' skates. When this warm top layer freezes, it creates a smooth ice surface. Cold water is not used because it would freeze too quickly and create bumps and air bubbles in the ice. The ideal temperature for this water is around 140°F (60°C).

The quality of ice definitely impacts how the game is played. Players tend to play a more conservative game, making safe plays rather than plays that require more finesse,

The Rink

The ice rink itself has changed little since the inception of the modern game. The dimensions of the hockey rinks that were established in Canada in the 1870s have not changed. The appearance and layout of the rink, however, have changed during the following decades.

Today's ice rink is surrounded by a series of "boards" that not only keep the puck in play but also offer a backboard for passing the puck. The boards average 3 feet (1m) high. In addition, on top of the boards, a second wall of shatterproof, clear plastic extends upward and is called the "glass." High netting is also used around the scoring ends of the rink to prevent the puck from flying into the stands.

Two blue lines, each 12 inches (30cm) wide, divide the playing surface into three separate and equally-sized zones. These are called the defending, offensive, and neutral zones. The distance between the goal to the first line is 60 feet (18m), while 10 feet (3m) separates the goal line from the boards surrounding the ice.

At each end of the hockey rink, there is a metal frame holding a cloth net, which serves as the goal. The dimensions of the net itself are 6 feet by 4 feet (1.8m by 1.2m). In front of the net is the goal crease, the area where the goaltender stays during games to defend the net from opposing players. This area has a 6-foot (1.8m) radius, is outlined by thin red lines, and is painted blue. Invasion of the goal crease by an opposing player is called interference and results in a penalty.

THE LAYOUT OF THE MODERN RINK

The dimensions of the ice hockey rink have changed little over the years, but the layout has adapted as the game has evolved.

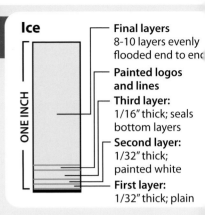

Ice

ONE INCH

Final layers
8-10 layers evenly flooded end to end

Painted logos and lines

Third layer:
1/16" thick; seals bottom layers

Second layer:
1/32" thick; painted white

First layer:
1/32" thick; plain

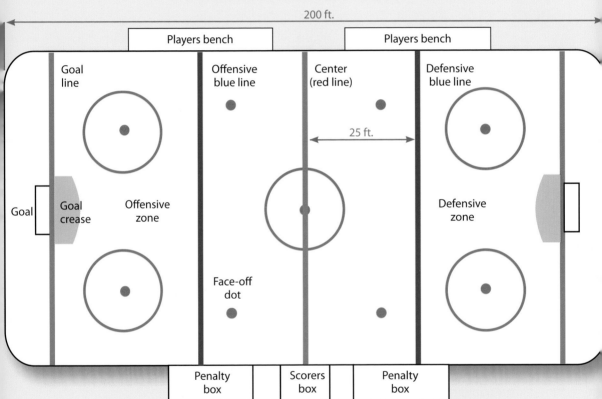

200 ft.

Players bench

Players bench

Goal line

Offensive blue line

Center (red line)

Defensive blue line

25 ft.

Goal

Goal crease

Offensive zone

Defensive zone

Face-off dot

Penalty box

Scorers box

Penalty box

when the ice is slower. Fast or hard ice is simply easier to skate on and allows the player to make more precise turns.

Hockey players know which arenas have the best ice. Canadian hockey rinks, for instance, are well-known for the high quality of their ice. The colder Canadian climate plays a significant role in this, as rinks in warmer climates tend to "melt" faster, creating impurities in the ice surface.

Skating on Vibrating Molecules

Chemist Gabor Somorjai discovered that a person actually skates on vibrating molecules. Journalist Kirsten Weir explains, "Like all matter, ice is composed of particles called molecules. At the surface of the ice, the molecules exist in a part-solid, part-liquid state. That quasi-liquid layer makes ice slick."[12]

For years, scientists believed that friction (rubbing one object against another) and pressure caused the ice to melt, thus providing a slicker surface which enabled skaters to glide more efficiently. Somorjai discovered that skates and pucks did not create enough pressure to cause melting. Instead, the quasi liquid layer of ice created by the vibrating molecules was sufficient to keep the ice slick.

This layer of quasi liquid ice is thin. A warmer ice rink, however, adds depth to this layer and creates slower ice. With additional layers, the ice becomes slushy, creating more friction that slows down the players. This is one reason why ice rinks are kept so cold. At warmer temperatures, too much melting occurs.

How Skates Work

Putting pressure on ice by standing or skating across it melts a thin layer of ice. As the ice melts and creates water, the ice surface becomes slippery. When combined with the pressure or rubbing of a skate against the ice, the friction between the ice and the skate is greatly reduced. This allows the skater to easily glide across the ice. Weir explains, "Very little friction exists between ice and skates."[13] Friction is the force resisting motion on solid surfaces. The larger the object moving along a solid surface, the greater the friction and the less quickly that object moves. According to scientists, "the friction between the [skate] blade and the ice is minimized because the surface of the ice is so slippery, and because only a small portion of the skate's blade is actually in contact."[14]

Skates Through the 1800s

The word *skate* comes from the Dutch word *schaat*, meaning skaters. The first ice skates were created around 3000 B.C. and were made of animal bones. The bones were tied to the bottoms of shoes with some form of rope, but were unreliable because the rope would often loosen, causing the bones to fall off. To correct this problem, the Dutch created wooden skates in the fourteenth century; these were slightly more effective and less prone to falling off. The wood, however, did not always glide well across the

Nineteenth-century ice skates. Iron skate blades, called stock skates, replaced older versions made of bone and wood because the iron absorbed less water from the ice.

ice, and the wood absorbed moisture and made the skates heavy.

Eventually iron blades replaced bone and wooden blades. Iron blades were thinner and sharper, leaving a smaller surface actually in contact with the ice which created less friction between the blades and the ice. They also did not absorb water from the ice like bone and wooden blades did. An ice skater screwed this skate onto the sole of his boot; because the screws sometimes came loose straps made of leather or rope were also used to hold the skates securely to the foot. Called stock skates, these skates were used in the 1800s.

Skates in the 1900s and Today

Despite the reduced friction that allowed easier gliding, stock skates would often loosen and come off while the individual was moving. This severely limited the kind of skating people could do.

The primary producer of stock skates was the Starr Manufacturing Company of Nova Scotia, Canada, which opened in 1866. After numerous complaints about the durability of their skates, inventor John Forbes of Starr, along with his assistant, Thomas Bateman, began to work on improving the skates. What players wanted was an all-metal, self-fastening skate. Forbes and Bateman came up with the Acme Club Skate, a skate that did not require leather strapping. Instead, the Acme clamped onto a boot with a lever that was adjustable to any foot size. These skates were first sold in 1865. Because of its affordability and durability, the Acme Club Skate was soon selling throughout North America. Many historians credit this scientific invention with changing the face of ice hockey and increasing its popularity in the late nineteenth century. Finally the skating world had a skate with a blade that would not detach from the boot, improving the quality of skating.

Different Types of Skates

Ice hockey skates are different than figure skating skates. While both skates have a hollow area between two sharp edges, in figure skating, the skater uses only one edge at a time so as to create a smoother glide on the ice. Hockey players use both edges. In addition, figure skaters have a large set of jagged teeth on the front of the blade, called a toe pick. These are used in jumping and intricate footwork.

A KIND HELPER.

A women helps put on skates with leather strapping. The Acme Club Skate, which clamped onto a boot instead of using straps, was easier to put on and was more durable.

Starr Manufacturing closed in 1938 but by that time the company had produced more than 11 million pairs of skates. A lighter pair of skates called tube skates was introduced in 1900. This skate was made of steel and was screwed directly onto a skating boot. The skating boot was designed with extra support for the ankle in order to prevent the ankle from twisting and turning and being injured during the game. Today's hockey skates have steel blades and a rigid boot that helps protect the player's ankles and feet.

A goaltender's skates are slightly different. They are made with a special feature called a puck stop. This is a triangular extension that helps stop the puck from passing through the space between the boot and the blade.

Made of Steel

Today skate blades are made of steel. While the blades look flat, they are, in fact, concave or curved and hollowed inwardly. Team equipment managers use a process called hollow grinding that produces two sharp edges on the skate with a hollowed-out area in the center. Hockey journalist Finn Erickson explains, "The function of the hollow is to increase or decrease the grip of the blade on the ice surface." According to Bill Willis, a teacher at Worsley School in Worsley, Alberta, Canada, "[the] shallow depression [hollow] allows the edges of the blade on either side to bite into the ice…. This prevents the skate from sliding sideways … giving the player more stability." Each hockey player has his own preference about sharpness and the amount of hollow he wants on his skates. Goalies generally prefer less hollow because they are not required to do the stopping and starting that other players need to make.

The equipment manager is responsible for sharpening and maintaining the team's skates. He or she uses a blade sharpener that has a rotating stone wheel that is capable of creating the hollow part of the skate. The skate blade is passed over the stone wheel to smooth and sharpen the blade. A final pass is made using a light coat of oil to give the blade more polish and smoothness.

Sharp skates are necessary to prevent a player from "losing an edge." When a

Skates today are made of steel and hollowed inwardly to give the player more stability.

blade becomes dull, players will sometimes have their skates come out from under them, resulting in a fall. Losing an edge can occur because of a skate's contact with dirt or sand off the ice or because of contact with another skate blade during a collision. When this happens, a player often returns to the locker room for a brief period to have his skate blade resharpened.

Finn Erickson, "Some Facts About Skate Sharpening and the Effects It Can Have on Your Skating," *Pure Hockey the Magazine*.

Bill Willis, "Ice Skate Blades," Worsley School Online, www.worsleyschool.net/science/files/skate/blades.html.

Skating and Speed

Proper skates and the slippery surface of the ice allow players to generate speed while skating. The sharp edge of the skate digs into the ice, creating traction or pulling power; this allows the player to accelerate quickly. Because ice is slippery, the digging in of the skate provides a solid contact with the ice, thus preventing the skates from slipping and providing the player with a quick start. It also allows the player to stop quickly. To stop, most hockey players scrape the ice with the edges of their skates; this creates friction which helps in slowing down the player.

Professional ice hockey players have been known to reach speeds up to 25 miles per hour (40kmh) on the ice. Some players are faster than others, depending on their strength and efficiency on the ice.

According to physicist Thomas Humphrey, skating is "the fastest way to travel on the surface of the earth on your feet."[15] When running, a person is slowed down by his or her feet touching the ground; this creates a large amount of friction between the runner's shoes and the ground. In skating, because there is very little friction between the blade and the ice, players can glide across the ice and build up speed as they skate. Speed is the measure of distance traveled in time. Several speed skaters have been clocked at over 30 miles an hour (48kmh.) In comparison, speed runners run around 23 miles per hour (37kmh.)

According to ice hockey expert and trainer Laura Stamm, speed is

> affected by a combination of several elements: proper skating technique, power (pushing correctly and with explosive force), and leg speed (quickness.) A combination of all these elements can yield an explosively fast skater.... Every skating maneuver has a two-fold weight shift on every stride—first from pushing skate/leg to gliding skate/leg, and then from gliding skate/leg to pushing skate/leg. The ability to shift weight properly and at the right instance is an extremely important element [in skating with speed].[16]

When players dig their skates into the ice to accelerate, they also lean forward, exerting a strong force on their legs and hips. Gravity then pulls down the player's body mass which gives him better traction on the ice; this helps propel him forward. In addition, a player's arms and shoulders are important in skating because they help the body maintain balance; they act as a counterbalance to the legs and feet and provide more equilibrium.

Crossovers

When a player skates on a curve, it is called a crossover. According to Stamm, the term *crossover* refers to "the passing of the outside skate over (in front of) the toe of the inside skate.... [Crossovers] make it possible for players to generate speed for the straight-aways, to weave in and out of traffic, to zigzag down the ice, change direction, turn from backward to forward, and move laterally (from side to side) and to fake."[17] These moves are an essential part of hockey.

A crossover, passing the outside skate over the toe of the inside skate, helps a hockey player generate speed, change directions, weave, and move laterally.

Centripetal force is the scientific principle that enables the player to skate in a circular path. Centripetal force is the tendency of objects in rotation to move inward toward the center, or axis, of rotation due to gravity, or the force of attraction between objects. An example of centripetal force occurs when someone whirls a stone around by a string. The person's hands exert an inner pull or centripetal force on the stone in order to keep it moving.

In hockey a player relies on the same inner pull when turning a corner. Stamm explains,

> Skating on circles and curves ... involves powerful forces that tend to oppose the skater's desired directionality. Centripetal force is the force that keeps the player skating in a circular path.... Centripetal force is created by the blades thrusting against the ice (toward the center of the circle) at a strong angle. As the skater's lower body (skates, knees, hips) lean inward ... gravitational forces work to make the skater fall. The object of the skater is to keep the curve tight and to minimize wasted distance ... while remaining upright and balanced.... The entire lower body ... leans into the circle at a strong angle. To prevent a fall, the upper body ... must be situated directly above the center of gravity [located directly above the skates].... To balance over the center of gravity, the skater must "counter-lean" with the upper body. By counter-leaning, the upper body will be situated above the center of gravity. The lower body can now safely lean into the circle to skate the circle or curve.[18]

Thus, the weight shift is from the inside to the outside of the skates, rather than from front to back. This shift in weight helps the skater to remain upright.

In addition to speed and centripetal force, velocity is also a factor in crossovers. Speed measures the rate at which a person or object travels, while velocity also includes direction. In motion that occurs in a straight line (rectilinear) speed and velocity are the same. On the other hand, when motion occurs along a curve, as it does in crossovers, the velocity is always changing because the direction of velocity is different. This change in velocity can affect balance as players make their quick turns on the ice; thus the player must move his body in the proper way to maintain control and equilibrium.

Some hockey players are able to perform such maneuvers more easily than others. Learning to balance various body parts takes lots of practice but can result in much quicker skating and maneuvering.

Checking and Collisions

Ice hockey is quite a physical sport. Checking, or colliding with another player in an effort to slow him down or affect his ability to play the game, is what makes hockey a collision sport. The scientific laws of motion and momentum play a significant role in checking and collisions on the ice.

Motion is the change of position or location of an object with respect to time. Momentum, as opposed to motion, is a measure of the amount of motion of an object. Science has

Ice hockey allows players to body check (collide with) an opponent in an attempt to slow him down or affect his playing ability.

shown that any free-moving object will travel in a straight line unless some force acts upon it. This is the foundation of the laws of motion, first recognized by Sir Isaac Newton (1642–1727).

Newton was an English physicist, astronomer, and philosopher who developed a number of scientific principles. Considered one of the most influential scientists in history, Newton is best known for his work on understanding gravity and the laws of motion.

There are three laws of motion. The law of inertia states that an object's speed and direction will remain constant unless acted upon by outside influences. When a force of some kind strikes an object, the law of constant acceleration comes into play. This law holds that the object will accelerate in the direction of the force and in proportion to the strength of that force. The third law is the law of conservation of momentum. This concept, which comes into effect during collisions of two objects, states that if a force is applied to an object, the object will react with an opposite and equal force.

To determine momentum, an object's mass must be multiplied by its velocity. The mass of the object is always constant; in order to change momentum, it is necessary to change the velocity. Thus, an object can be slowed down or sped up in its flight by changing its direction. Momentum, therefore, is dependent upon both the velocity and mass of a moving object, as is the force created when two objects collide.

These laws come into play in hockey when players "check" each other. Checking is the use of physical force to disrupt the opposition's play or to gain possession of the puck. A body check is when one player intentionally slams into another player, especially one with the puck, so that the other player loses control of the puck or is unable to advance toward the goal.

While most checking involves knocking an opposing player into the boards, some checking results in collisions between two fast-moving players. Stopping force is the force that is necessary to change the state of motion of a body.

The following example illustrates what a collision would be like between two real-life hockey players: Ottawa Senator player Daniel Alfredsson is moving about 20 miles an hour (32kmh) down the ice on his way to shoot the puck. His opponent, St. Louis Blues' player Keith Tkachuk, is determined to stop him and heads toward Alfredsson while moving 15 miles an hour (24kmh.) Alfredsson weighs 200 pounds (91kg), while Tkachuk weighs 220 (100kg). A collision between these two players would result in a little over 5,800 joules, a metric measure of energy. This creates a stopping force of 666 pounds (302kg) and enough energy to light a 60-watt light bulb for ninety-six seconds.

Each player will experience the same tremendous force in the collision, because, according to Newton's third law, for

Most checking in ice hockey involves knocking an opponent into the boards.

every action there is an equal and opposite reaction. At least one player will end up falling on the ice, maybe both. There is also a good chance that one or both players will be injured simply because of the tremendous impact between them.

This kind of collision is legal in hockey. The only time a penalty is called is when one player blindsides another player who does not have the puck. This occurs when one player is not watching or does not see the approach of the other and is unable to prepare for the collision. Penalties are also called for sending an opposing player into the boards headfirst.

All hockey collisions can result in injuries. These injuries occur because of the tremendous force that is created by the collision.

CHAPTER 3

Flexibility, Speed, and Reaction Time: Controlling the Puck

Many of the scientific principles that come into play while skating, such as friction, gravity, energy, and momentum, are also factors in shooting and stopping the puck. Momentum, for instance, comes into play when players take certain shots with their hockey sticks, as well with the movement of the puck. Speed and velocity also play a large role in these actions, as does the reaction time of the goaltender.

Flexibility of the players and of their hockey sticks also affect shooting the puck. Reaction time, the time it takes a person to react to an outside stimulus, comes into play in the goaltender's ability to stop a flying puck from entering the net. With shots coming at high speed toward the net, a goaltender must react within seconds or suffer the indignity of an opponent scoring a goal.

The Puck

Like ice skates, the hockey puck has undergone many changes in its history. In the early days of hockey, any round object was used as a puck. Native Americans played the game with a painted or carved wooden ball and, in some cases, with a simple piece of wood.

Early ice hockey players generally used a ball rather than a puck, but they soon found that the ball was too active and bounced too much on a hard ice surface. This made scoring more difficult because the ball was so hard to control. As a result, many players cut off the top and bottom of a round ball to give it flat surfaces.

Today a standard ice hockey puck is black and measures 1-inch (2.5cm) thick and 3 inches (7.6cm) in diameter. It weighs about 6 ounces (170g). There is no particular reason why pucks are black other than easy visibility on a clear ice surface. Other colors and weights are used at different levels of hockey, as well as during practice sessions. As far as the thickness is concerned, a thicker and heavier puck would be more dangerous for the players in terms of potential injury, whereas a thinner or lighter one would not be heavy enough to travel with any degree of accuracy.

Many National League teams use as many as five thousand pucks a year; thirty to forty pucks, are used in each game. It is widely believed that the word *puck* derives from the Gaelic word *puc* or the Irish word *poc*, meaning to punch or poke.

Pucks are made of vulcanized rubber. Vulcanization is a chemical process that uses high pressure and high temperature to convert rubber into more durable materials. Huge batches of rubber are mixed with coal dust and then put into machines that make a roll of rubber shaped like a giant sausage. A slicer is then used to cut the rubber roll into pucks; they are then placed in molds and the team's logo is glued onto the back. Then the pucks are cooked at a high temperature (about 300°F [150°C]) for about twenty minutes. Hockey pucks

POWER PLAY

Over 100 miles per hour

Speed that a slap shot can travel

are made in only a few countries, notably Canada, Russia, the Czech Republic, China, and Slovakia.

Pucks are frozen prior to game use to reduce the potential for bouncing during play and to make them slide better. Scientist Andrew Franz explains, "Rubber possesses a high potential for friction, especially when wet.... A warm puck, or even a room temperature puck, will heat the ice and halt it abruptly from its desired path. However, when a puck is frozen, friction is reduced and the puck slides more regularly."[19]

Freezing decreases bouncing by hardening the rubber, thus giving the puck less yield. Rubber is a soft substance made up of long polymers (large molecules with many structural units) that have elastic properties; they are able to stretch and then return to previous size and shape. Freezing the rubber reduces the ability of the molecules to stretch, making the puck less prone to bouncing.

Hockey pucks, made of vulcanized rubber, are only manufactured in a few countries, including this factory in the Czech Republic.

While small in size, pucks can be very dangerous for a hockey player who gets hit by one. Pucks can reach speeds over 100 miles an hour (161kmh) when they are struck by a stick on the ice. Players who get struck by a flying puck can suffer from lacerations, broken bones, and concussions. Spectators are also occasionally injured. The most serious incident took place in March 2002 when a thirteen-year-old girl died two days after being hit in the head by a flying puck in a National Hockey League game in Columbus, Ohio.

Partly as a result of this incident, Plexiglas panels that sit atop the boards to protect spectators have been supplemented with large mesh nets that extend higher in the air. In addition, prior to each hockey game, fans are warned by the arena announcer about the possibility of pucks flying into

The Hockey Puck and Temperature

Once a puck is hit, its actions are governed by the scientific law of action-reaction. This means that when there is a collision between two objects (the stick making contact with the puck or the puck making contact with the boards), there is an equal force applied to both objects. The smaller object, in this case the puck, will accelerate.

The following experiment can be done at home to show the difference between a frozen puck and a warmer one:

1. Take two pucks (or two baseballs or two golf balls). Put one in the freezer and leave it there for two to three hours. Leave the other puck or ball at room temperature.
2. Find a cement surface that is relatively flat.
3. Drop the pucks or balls from waist level and watch how they bounce.
4. You will immediately notice that the room-temperature puck or ball bounces higher than the frozen one.
5. Throw the pucks or balls up in the air and allow them to bounce. Once again, observe the difference between the two.

Why does the warm puck or ball bounce higher? A warm object is more flexible. Because of this, the energy stored within it is released more quickly and effectively than with the frozen object.

Science of Hockey, "Shooting the Puck," Science of Hockey, www.exploratorium.edu/hockey/shooting1.html.

the spectator area. Fans are urged to watch the puck to avoid potential injury.

The Hockey Stick

A hockey stick is an essential tool for all ice hockey players and is used to shoot, pass, and propel the puck across the ice. On average, and depending on a player's height, sticks are usually 5 to 6.5 feet (1.5m to 2m) long and are composed of a long shaft with a flat extension at the end, called the blade. The blade is the only part of the stick that comes in contact with the puck.

The blade is attached to the stick at an angle of around 135 degrees, giving the stick an L-shape appearance. This angle is dependent in part on a player's height. The Hockey

In the early days of ice hockey, most hockey sticks were made of wood.

Stick Experts Web site explains, "Players usually seek a lie [an angle of the blade] that will put their blade flat on the ice while they are in their typical skating stance."[20] By having the blade flat on the ice, a hockey player has more control of the puck.

In the early days of ice hockey, most hockey sticks were made of wood. The earliest players often used sturdy limbs from trees and fashioned their own sticks. The first manufactured sticks were made by the Starr Manufacturing Company, which patented a stick called the Mic-Mac, named in honor of early Native American players of the Micmac tribe. The stick was made from yellow birch. These early sticks were heavy to use and not very flexible.

Next to be used was the laminated wooden stick, which came into use in the 1940s. Lamination is the process of uniting two or more layers of material together. These sticks were, thus, made of layers of wood that had been glued together in the hopes of creating a more flexible, yet durable, piece of equipment. When stress or force is applied, as it is in shooting a puck, to a stick made from one single piece of wood, the wood absorbs the entire amount of stress and is subject to breaking. The layered wood, on the other hand, creates a sturdier stick because the applied stress is spread out among the different layers, leading to less breakage.

During the 1960s, many companies began adding a layer of fiberglass to improve the stick's durability. Fiberglass is a material made from fine fibers of glass and is used as a reinforcing agent with other materials. It was also at this time that the blade of the stick became curved. In the 1970s aluminum was used for the first time in stick composition. A hockey stick made of aluminum has a hollow shaft, making it more lightweight. At the same time, aluminum also has more flexible properties that allow the stick to bend without breaking.

Today there are a variety of materials used in the composition of hockey sticks. The Science of Hockey Web site states, "There are now aluminum shafts, graphite shafts, and even sticks and blades that are entirely made of carbon-graphite. Graphite, carbon-graphite, and aluminum shafts provide strength and generally weigh less than wooden sticks."[21] These newer materials are made of elements that are lighter than wood; a 6-foot (1.8m) length of wood weighs a lot more than a similar length of aluminum or carbon-graphite.

In addition, the newer sticks are manufactured with more flexible properties. Scientist Angus McLean explains, "Hockey sticks are now designed to flex at certain zones along the shaft."[22] There are actually built-in flex patterns in the stick; rather than stress or energy being focused in one place, it is spread throughout the stick, creating a stronger and more durable piece of equipment. While these sticks are a big improvement over earlier sticks, they are also much more expensive to make. Most hockey players today play with composite sticks, although a few still favor the wooden ones.

When a player hits the puck, his stick bends forward to create more power; energy is created by this action and causes

Since hockey sticks occasionally break, most hockey players have several backup sticks.

the puck to accelerate. The Hockey Stick Expert Web site explains, "When a player bends his hockey stick when taking a shot, it essentially turns the hockey stick into a spring storing energy. When the spring is released (when the stick unbends and returns to straight), the energy is released and accelerates the puck."[23] The older sticks absorbed too much energy during the shot and often broke; today's sticks do not absorb as much energy so they are less prone to breaking. It takes a tremendous force for sticks to break. According to the Science of Hockey Web site, in one experiment "it took nearly one ton of force to break ... [the] hockey stick."[24]

Despite the improvements, however, hockey sticks do break on occasion. The energy transfer when a player hits the puck, for instance, may be slightly off center causing the stick to shatter. This occurs when a player hits the ice too far behind the puck creating stronger than normal force on the stick, which causes it to break. For this reason, most hockey players have several backup sticks with them at every game.

A goalie's stick is slightly different than those used by his teammates. It is wider throughout and widens even further into a paddlelike blade to give the goalie an even wider surface area which he can use to stop the puck from going into the goal.

Individual Sticks and Blades

Professional players typically have contracts with the companies that make hockey sticks and purchase those that have been made especially for them. Sticks are designated as either right or left-handed, depending on whether a player shoots with his right or left hand; the blade curves accordingly in the same direction. For instance, if a player is a right-handed shooter, he will place his right hand one third of the way down the shaft and hold the end of the stick with his left hand when making a shot.

Another factor that affects a player's selection is the amount of flexibility he wants in the stick. For the most part, defensemen use a slightly stiffer stick; with less bend, they are better able to stick check their opponents and steal the puck. Forwards will usually use a more flexible shaft, which allows for quick and accurate wrist shots, as well as passing. In deciding on a stick's flexibility, a player also takes into account his size and weight. Stronger and heavier players generally prefer stiffer sticks that do not bend as much.

The top part of the stick is commonly wrapped with some kind of cloth tape that helps with the grip. The tape has adhesive on both sides; this makes it easier for the player to keep his grip on the stick. The blade is also wrapped with cloth tape. This is done to improve the handling of the puck as well as to prevent water damage to the blade. The type of

A Curved Blade

Until the 1960s, all hockey stick blades were straight. Then professional player Andy Bathgate of the New York Rangers began experimenting with his stick; he broke it to create a curve in the blade and found he could make his slap shots more effective. Other players soon discovered how effective a curved stick could be by mistake. Player Bobby Hull of the Chicago Blackhawks, for instance, caught his stick in some wood around the rink, breaking it. He, too, found the broken stick more effective. In an interview with the *Kansas City Star*, Alain Haché, author of *The Physics of Hockey*, explains, "The curve is not about speed. It is more about accuracy and puck control. It's more about having a shot that leaves the blade at a more consistent point. That allows the shot to have more accuracy.... A curved stick gives stability to the puck." As word spread about the effectiveness of a curved stick, more and more players began asking their

equipment managers to put a curve in the stick blades they used.

The curve of a hockey stick refers to the amount the blade curves from toe to heel (front to back). There are several different types of curves used by hockey players. One of the most common is the toe curve, where the curve is concentrated in the toe or front end of the stick blade; this curve enables a player to handle the puck better and leads to more accurate wrist shots. A heel curve is more effective in slap shots.

Another differentiation is whether the stick blade is open or closed. An open blade means the face of the blade is turned up more sharply; this creates a higher trajectory (the path of a moving object through space) on shots. The opposite is true of closed blades.

Quoted in Pete Grathoff, "Control, Not Power, Is the Reason for a Curved Hockey Stick," *Kansas City Star*, December 20, 2009, www.kansascity.com/2009/12/20/1642256_control-not-power-is-reason-for.html.

CURVED BLADES AND CONTROL

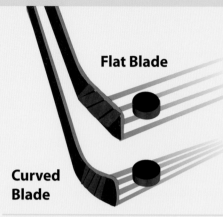

Flat Blade

Curved Blade

Over the years, many hockey players have found that using a curved blade allows for better control in their shooting. Today, blades come in a variety of shapes, designed to improve a player's ability to handle, pass, and shoot the puck.

Different Blade Shapes

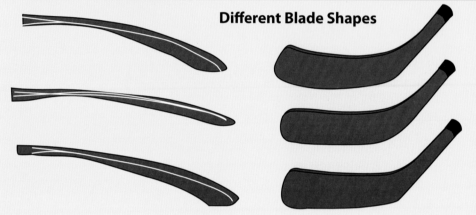

tape used is water-resistant and keeps the blade from direct contact with the ice surface. It also allows better contact with the puck due to a dry surface; dryness allows a more direct and controlled hit. The tape also provides a rough surface which is less slippery than a smooth one; this helps to create a straighter shot with less slipping off the center or toe of the blade.

Most players use black tape because of its visibility; others prefer white because it blends in with the ice and is less visible from afar. The decision on which color tape to use is up to the players.

The Slap Shot

Better sticks and blades have made shooting the puck easier and more efficient. One of the most effective of all hockey shots is the slap shot; it is momentum, motion, and speed that make this shot difficult to stop. Pucks, hit by such a shot, can travel at speeds up to 100 miles an hour (161kmh). This is one of the fastest shots in sports, although tennis balls and golf balls exceed the speed of a hockey puck. This shot is also one of the most exciting shots in the game of hockey.

Every year before the National Hockey League All-Star game, the players participate in various competitions. These include speed skating, shooting the puck, and various maneuvering skills. Boston Bruins player Zdeno Chara set a new skills competition record for the fastest slap shot at the 2008–09 All-Star game when his shot was clocked at 105.4 miles per hour (169.6kmh). At that speed, the puck reached the net in less than 0.4 seconds.

During a slap shot the stick bends and then snaps back into position, which releases energy into the puck and creates more power in the shot.

Most scientists believe that the slap shot is all about technique and energy transfer. This is what creates the power behind the shot. Journalist Kirsten Weir explains,

THE MOTION BEHIND THE SLAP SHOT

A slap shot is widely considered to be the fastest shot in ice hockey.

1 To perform this shot, the player first twists his or her torso, raising the stick and then bringing it down. This creates angular momentum which transfers energy to the puck.

2 Most players connect with the ice a foot before they reach the puck, which creates a bend in the hockey stick. This gives the puck more energy when the blade makes contact and snaps back into alignment.

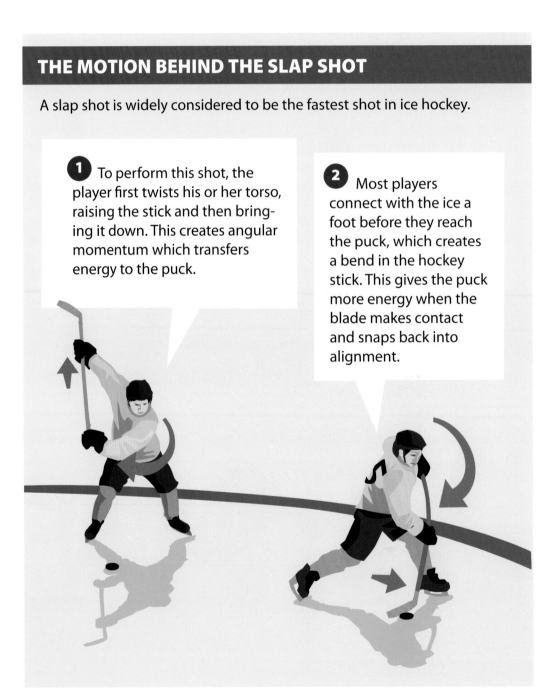

To prepare for the slap shot, a player twists at the waist as he swings the stick backward, then forward. That twisting action creates angular momentum, the momentum of a rotating object. The more momentum an object has, the harder it is to stop [and the faster it goes.] As the player strikes the puck, that angular momentum changes into linear momentum, driving the puck forward in a straight line.[25]

During a slap shot, most players hit the ice about 12 inches (30cm) behind the puck with their stick and then sweep it forward to make contact. When the stick first comes in contact with the ice, it bends because of its built-in flexibility. This bow or bend in the stick creates more power because when the stick snaps back into position at puck contact, it releases energy into the puck, causing faster speeds.

To make a slap shot, a player twists at the waist and shifts his weight from back to front; he also uses a wrist snap. This snap creates spin off the stick, like a coiled spring that snaps. This wrist snap essentially produces a rotating action that keeps the puck stable in its flight and helps in accuracy.

In addition, the hockey stick absorbs less energy allowing more power to transfer to the puck. Weir explains, "Every time a player hits the puck, energy passes from the athlete to the stick to the puck."[26]

Other Shots

Other hockey shots are not quite as powerful as the slap shot. Another popular and effective shot is the wrist shot, made with a flick of the wrist. This shot is different than the slap shot in that it lacks the wind-up that is used in making the slap shot; in addition, the puck is in contact with the stick blade for a slightly longer period of time. This gives the player more control over the direction of the puck.

While the wrist shot is not as powerful as the slap shot, it is often more accurate. Players can generally place this shot closer to where they actually want it to go. Sports columnist Dan Peterson explains, "To send the puck into … the goal, a player must be able to control not only its horizontal direction but also its height when aiming at the top corners [of the net]."[27]

Longer stick contact makes this possible. The puck is aimed with the follow-through of the stick; the puck will generally fly in the direction of the extension of the stick, accounting for more accuracy.

The one-timer is another shot that has the potential to be hit with a lot of power. This shot occurs when one player passes the puck to another and a shot is made immediately by the second player. In this case, the second player winds up before the puck arrives and then quickly redirects the puck toward the net. Capable of nearly reaching the speed of a slap shot, the one-timer shot is difficult to stop because of the quickness with which it is hit. The rapid change in direction not only adds extra energy to the shot but is also often hard for the goalie to follow.

Stopping the Puck

The goaltender is responsible for stopping all shots before they enter the net. A goalie has a number of ways he can stop the puck. The most common way is stopping it with his body, resulting in the puck bouncing off his padding and away from the net. He can also use his oversize catching glove to actually catch the puck or he can reject the puck with his stick.

All of these methods require speed and agility on the part of the goaltender. Reaction time and mental preparation are the key components for a successful goaltender. The Science of Hockey Web sites states, "In a game where the puck travels at high speeds, the difference between a goal and a save can come down to milliseconds."[28]

Many players believe that the best goaltenders have natural ability and quickness. Many scientists agree, arguing that reaction time is a genetic trait. However, most goaltenders, with or without this genetic trait, can improve their ability to react quickly through practice.

In such a high-speed sport as hockey, a goalie's reflexes are also key in protecting the goal. If a puck is shot from the blue line, which is 60 feet (18m) away from the goal, at 100 miles per hour (161kmh), the puck will reach the goaltender in 0.4 seconds. This does not allow the goalie much time to block the shot. Several factors can impact the goaltender's success and improve his reaction time. The first is just being in the right place at the right time. Sometimes, this is the result of luck, but usually it is because the goaltender is paying attention to where the puck is at all times.

Pucks often travel faster than the naked eye can track. It is, therefore, amazing that most goaltenders are able to stop nearly 90 percent of the shots that are directed at the goal.

Science writer Charles Q. Choi explains, "To do this, the best athletes rely on what researcher Joan Vickers at the University of Calgary dubbed the quiet eye, the critical moment of focus prior to action."[29]

To observe this phenomenon, researchers inserted a camera in goaltenders' helmets and followed their eye movements during a game. According to Choi, the researchers discovered that "elite goalies focused directly on the puck nearly a full second before the shot was released nearly three-quarters of the time. They also concentrated on the ice in front of the stick when it came to a quarter of all shots. Their gaze was only on the body of the shooter two percent of the time."[30]

This ability to see the puck before a shot is taken shortens the reaction time and allows the goaltender to stop a speeding puck. Researchers also found that new or novice goaltenders allowed their eyes to wander over the ice; this lessened

Vancouver Canucks goalie Roberto Luongo stretches for a puck. A goalie's reflexes and ability to see the puck at all times are key factors in being able to prevent a goal.

their chances of stopping the puck. Thus, experience and practice play a significant role in the ability of goaltenders to prevent scoring.

To be at their best, goaltenders also have to be well prepared mentally. During pregame warm up drills, goalies practice taking shots from their teammates. Concentrating on preventing the pucks from reaching the goal helps the goalies sharpen their mental faculties They also "stop" imaginary shots by crouching down in front of the net and moving from side to side. This further sharpens their mental processes.

Each goalie also has his or her own special ritual prior to the start of a game. These rituals include touching a helmet in a special way and using a stick to touch all four corners of the net. Goalies say their ritual helps them attain the proper mental focus that is needed to play their position.

Another factor that can help goalies be more effective is the concept of being "in the zone." Players whose abilities seem heightened or extremely sharp during a game are often

Reaction Time

Professional goaltenders have amazing reaction times. With pucks reaching the net in milliseconds, a goaltender must be alert and ready to react throughout the game. You can measure your own reaction time with the following experiment. You'll need a friend to help you out.

Find a wooden yardstick. Rest your arm on the edge of a table, with your hand hanging over the edge. Holding your thumb and index finger about an inch apart, have your friend hold the yardstick so that its bottom edge is located between your fingers. Without warning, have your friend drop the yardstick. See how fast you can react and close your fingers on the stick.

Most people are able to catch the yardstick at around the 6-inch (15cm) mark. You can use the following table to gauge your reaction time:

Distance the Yardstick Falls	Reaction Time
5 inches	0.16 seconds
6 inches	0.18 seconds
7 inches	0.19 seconds
8 inches	0.20 seconds

Science of Hockey, "Making Saves," Science of Hockey, www.exploratorium.edu/hockey/save1.html.

described as being in the zone. Many goalies and other athletes describe this as a feeling of being invulnerable, of always being in the right place at the right time, and of playing at a level not previously achieved.

A quarterback who is in the zone, for instance, may complete dozens of passes, a goalie who doesn't allow one goal in a whole game, or a golfer might shoot the lowest round of his career. None of these athletes will be able to describe exactly how he achieved this high level of success. He was just "in the zone" when nothing went wrong and everything went right.

CHAPTER **4**

Safety Gear and Injuries: Protecting the Players

Despite many improvements in the game and the equipment, injuries in ice hockey cannot be avoided entirely. Almost every professional and amateur ice hockey player will experience an injury at some point in his or her career. While many injuries are caused by fouls or rough play, others are caused by falls, collisions, and simple wear and tear on the body. The Sports Injury Clinic, an Internet site that provides information on a wide variety of sports injuries and treatment, states, "Ice hockey is one of the most dangerous and injury heavy sports. This is due to the combination of fast speeds, multiple collisions, long hockey sticks, a slippery playing surface, sharp blades, and a puck traveling up to 100 miles per hour."[31]

Many serious injuries can be avoided or lessened in their severity by the use of proper equipment. The various hockey associations around the world have mandated the use of certain equipment that greatly reduces the chance of serious injury. Such equipment includes goalie masks, helmets, mouth guards, and padding. All this equipment tends to be heavy. Tim Burt, manager of the Fairfax Ice Arena in Fairfax,

Virginia, describes the difference between today's equipment and that used in the past by hockey players: "The gear has gotten a lot lighter weight. The goal is to increase mobility and protection without increasing weight."[32]

Corry Kelahear, director of product management for the Hockey Company in Montreal, explains how today's equipment can prevent injury: "Dispersing the impact of a blow has been an important design aspect of protective gear. Certain areas of pads are reinforced, which takes the energy away from the joints and moves it toward the muscles. The muscles are better equipped to handle heavy impacts."[33]

Experts agree that modern equipment can help prevent injuries and lessen the severity of those that do occur. However, Dave Fischer, a spokesman for USA Hockey, which governs amateur play in the United States, says, "There's no foolproof way to protect any part of the body from injury."[34]

Protecting the Players

Because of the high risk of injury, all hockey players wear layers of protective gear. Shoulder pads, chest protectors, leg and shin guards, helmets, and gloves all help protect from possible injury. Of all the players on the ice, the goaltender is probably the most at risk due to his responsibility for stopping the puck. In the early days of hockey, goalies wore no protective equipment. This left them vulnerable to concussions, facial cuts, nasal fractures, and other injuries.

In the last several decades, however, innovations and changes in goalie equipment have made the goalie's job a bit easier. Designed to protect the goalie from the speed and dangers of the puck, the goalie's equipment is totally different than the rest of the players on the ice. Most goalie equipment weighs around 50 pounds (23kg,) as compared to the 20 pounds (9kg) worn by other players.

A goaltender's pads, for instance, are much thicker than those worn by his teammates, because the goalie faces the majority of shots. In addition the goalie wears large pads on his legs on top of his hockey uniform that reach nearly to

his groin. Oversize gloves protect the hands catching and blocking the puck. Goalies also have large helmets with face masks.

All hockey players wear protective gear such as chest protectors, leg guards, shin guards, helmets, and shoulder pads like the ones shown here.

According to hockey historian Douglas Hunter,

no [other] role in team sports has such violence associated with it. Injury, now much less a part of goaltending with advances in equipment, is an essential part of its lore.... The goaltender alone dresses for the worst. He is sheathed in more paraphernalia [protective gear] than a medieval knight, deliberately placing himself in the path of a chunk of vulcanized rubber hurtling at more than one hundred miles per hour.[35]

Goalies also wear skates with extra padding, a heavy chest protector, and heavy elbow and shoulder pads. This padding is

PROTECTIVE GEAR

Protective equipment has not always been embraced within the National Hockey League, but repeated serious injuries have resulted in a higher interest in player safety.

Player

Helmets

Mouthguards

Elbow Pads

Shoulder pads

Sticks

Gloves

Jocks

Pants

Girdles

Shin guards

Skates

Goalie

Masks

Chest Protectors

Sticks

Catchers

Blockers

Leg Pads

Pants

Skates

made out of synthetic materials which provide more strength and less absorbency than the old leather padding worn by hockey players of the past.

Evolution of the Goalie Mask

Until 1959, goaltenders did not wear masks. A facial injury to goaltender Jacques Plante compelled him to try a simple plastic shell to protect his face. Plastic masks soon led to the invention of a simple fiberglass one. Nearly thirty years would pass, however, before goalie masks became standard equipment.

One of the reasons for the slow acceptance of masks was the difficulty with which they were made. Goalies who wished to use a fiberglass mask had to undergo an uncomfortable procedure. Fiberglass had to be molded to the face; to accomplish this, a plaster impression of the face was necessary. Hunter explains, "Having a custom-fitted mask made meant subjecting yourself to the creation of a head mold. This entailed tugging a woman's stocking over your head, then being smeared with Vaseline and coated with plaster—and breathing through a straw so you didn't suffocate." When made, the fiberglass masks were white in color and rather plain in appearance. Goalies began painting their personal masks with different colors and symbols.

A serious eye injury to a Buffalo Sabres goalie who was wearing a fiberglass mask in 1977 helped start the movement toward a new and safer kind of mask. The birdcage mask, which is worn by goalies today, was developed in the 1970s. With a helmet made of fiberglass or Kevlar (the same mate-

The birdcage goalie mask worn today is often presonalized with decorations selected by that individual goalie.

rial used in bulletproof vests) and layers of internal padding, at least 0.63-inch (1.6cm) thick, covering the head, the mask part is similar to that worn by a baseball catcher. These masks and helmets offer solid protection from fast-flying pucks. Each top goalie in the National Hockey League has one or more personalized masks. Goalie Kelly Hrudey says, "The decorative paintings on the outside provide interest for the fans and help promote the game of hockey."

Douglas Hunter, A Breed Apart: *An Illustrated History of Goaltending*, Chicago: Benchmark, 1995, p. 127.

Quoted in Science of Hockey, "The Gear," Science of Hockey, www.exploratorium.edu/hockey/gear1.html.

The Bauer Nike Hockey company in Greenland, New Hampshire, manufactures much of the padding worn today by players and goalies. It makes the padding with a product called Dri-Fit. Journalist Jen Waters writes, "Dri-Fit … is a lining that wicks moisture away from the body. It keeps the player cooler throughout practices and games…. It is used inside gloves, pants, shin pads, shoulder pads, and elbow pads."[36] Dri-Fit and other similar products make use of water-repelling microfibers that are made of polyester and nylon. These fibers move moisture away from the skin where it can be evaporated in the air. The fibers are so small that moisture has a difficult time getting through them.

Goalie Masks

Perhaps no innovation in ice hockey has been as important as the goalie mask. Gary Abraham, a sports medicine specialist in youth hockey, says, "Goalies are more susceptible to injuries around the neck from pucks, skates, and sticks."[37] It took many years before players even considered wearing a protective mask and helmet.

In the early days of hockey, the goaltender was at high risk for injuries simply because of the lack of body and head protection. Fast-flying pucks that were not caught could easily cause facial lacerations, bruises, and other injuries. These injuries could also occur to other parts of the body as well. Collisions with other players who slid into the net could produce broken bones, while the skates of an out-of-control player could easily cause severe cuts. Goalies also had more concussions because of falls on the head or shots to the head. With as many as forty shots heading toward a goal during a game, goalie injuries were almost inevitable.

Clint Benedict, a Montreal Maroon goaltender, had his nose and cheekbone broken in 1930. After that he tried wearing a football face guard but found it hard to see through and around, and he eventually stopped wearing it. No other kind

of helmet or mask was used for the next twenty-nine years, although Benedict in later years as a hockey coach discovered a young goalie in Winnipeg named Roy Mosgrove who was using a wire-cage protector like catchers wear in baseball. Hunter writes, "It would take decades for the players … to see the wisdom of Roy Mosgrove, and to incorporate the wire cage into mask design."[38]

Jacques Plante of the Montreal Canadiens finally modernized the goalie's mask as a result of an injury he sustained. On November 1, 1959, Plante suffered a broken nose while blocking a shot from a New York Ranger player. Blood streamed down his face as he returned to the bench. Plante told his coach that he would no longer be playing goalie unless he could wear some kind of mask and protection. The coach allowed Plante to wear a thin skin-colored plastic shell to protect his face.

Plante's mask opened the door for future improvements. Since 1959, the goalie mask has undergone many changes.

Hockey Injuries

Hockey injuries are quite common, but just how common? On October 23, 2009, for instance, National Hockey League records indicate that seventy-six players were on the injured list. This was 11 percent of the 690 active players in the league.

Most injuries were minor and the players were expected to return to action in a matter of days. Several of the injuries, however, were more severe. Kari Lehtonen of the Atlanta Thrashers, for instance, suffered a back injury and was out for an indefinite period, while Adam Burish of the Chicago Blackhawks was sidelined with an injured knee and was listed as out until March 2010, as was Johan Franzen of the Detroit Red Wings who needed surgery to repair a torn ligament in his knee.

Eight different players were out for indefinite periods due to concussions or postconcussion syndrome. The only injury that was more common was knee injuries that accounted for twelve of the seventy-six injuries. Players unable to play due to injury can have a serious negative effect on a professional hockey team. Teams are forced to rely on minor league players to substitute for absent players. This can severely impact a team's performance and the chance of winning and making the playoffs.

Today's masks are both fashionable and practical. The newer masks and helmets are devised to protect not only the face, but also the ears and throat.

Common Injuries

Despite the many advances in hockey equipment, injuries still occur with alarming frequency. The most common injury in hockey is a simple laceration. Many hockey players suffer from various cuts to their body from impact with the puck, hockey stick, or skate. Sports medicine physicians estimate that almost half of all hockey injuries are lacerations.

Most of these injuries are treated by the team trainer and stitched in the dressing room during the game. Deeper cuts may require further treatment and more stitches. Kelly Sorensen, for instance, played hockey for the Hampton Roads Admirals, for a number of seasons. In three seasons, Sorensen needed over eighty stitches to close a variety of cuts. His teammate, Brendan Curley, needed one hundred during one season.

Another common ice hockey injury is a sprained or strained muscle. A sprain is an injury to a ligament, the tissue that holds bones together at the joints, whereas a strain is an injury to a muscle or tendon. Tendons connect muscle to bone; a tear in the tendon or muscle can be very painful.

Muscles are often bruised from a fall, a blow, or even a simple misstep. This results in a sprain, during which the ligaments that hold the bones together are torn. Numerous small blood vessels are also damaged which allows blood to get into the surrounding tissue, causing the area to swell. All strains and sprains are caused by excessive use or tension on a particular muscle or a blow that increases this tension.

Although the loss of teeth used to be more common in ice hockey, it is not unusual to see players with missing teeth.

Treatment of a sprain or strain is compression of the area with a tensor bandage and the application of ice. Both limit the amount of swelling. The tensor bandage also limits movement, allowing the torn muscle to repair itself.

Contusions, or bruises, are nearly everyday occurrences in ice hockey. A contusion or bruise is a discoloration of the skin caused by bleeding into the muscle or skin and follows a fall, hard hit, or other injury. They are treated with ice, compression, elevation, and rest.

Ice is applied every four hours for ten minutes at a time; ice causes the blood vessels to contract which slows down any bleeding into the tissue. It lessens swelling and inflammation by reducing the amount of fluid released from injured tissue that occurs automatically in response to an injury. The injured body part is also elevated to decrease swelling, as gravity will drain accumulated fluid away from the injury.

Lower back injuries are also part of hockey. Most involve some damage to the disc that lies between each vertebra. Discs rupture and can become compressed due to the bent-over position that hockey players skate and play in, along with their frequent collisions with other players and the board.

The loss of teeth used to be more common in ice hockey than it is today. Players now wear mouth guards that protect them from having teeth knocked out. Still, it is not unusual to see players with one or more teeth missing.

Facial cuts and fractures are also part of hockey. These have decreased somewhat in recent years due to more players wearing visors to protect part of their face. Visors are available; however, many players refuse to wear them because they say that the visors impair their vision.

Knee Injuries

Knee injuries occur frequently in ice hockey and are more serious than simple lacerations and strains. Richard Mangi, Peter Jokl, and O. William Dayton, authors of the book *Sports Fitness and Training*, explain, "Hockey is a rough game. The swift cuts and turns, the flying bodies, and sudden trips are unhealthy for ... knees."[39]

View of Knee

Human joints rely on a series of muscles, tendons, and ligaments to remain functional. In hockey, players must be careful to protect these areas to prevent painful, career-threatening injuries, such as a torn anterior cruciate ligament (ACL).

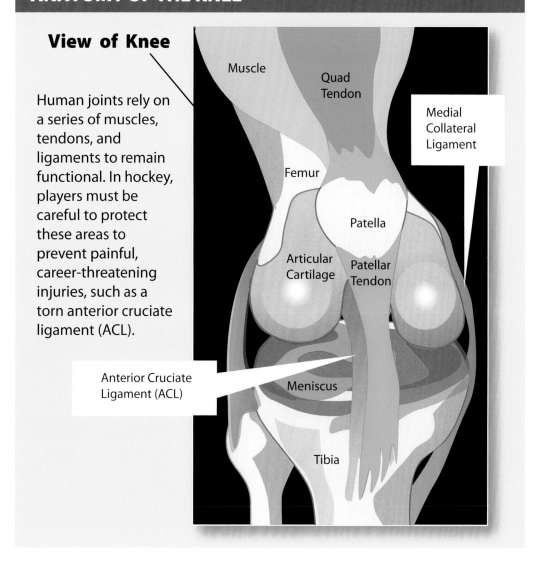

Muscle

Quad Tendon

Medial Collateral Ligament

Femur

Patella

Articular Cartilage

Patellar Tendon

Anterior Cruciate Ligament (ACL)

Meniscus

Tibia

The knee, which acts like a hinge, is designed to be flexible and provide stability for walking. The knee is where the major bones of the leg meet; the femur from above, and the tibia and fibula from below. The bones' meeting place is protected by another bone called the patella, or kneecap.

To provide further support, five thick ligaments hold the bones together. Another two ligaments, called the

POWER PLAY

cruciate ligaments, add stability. In addition, the knee is also filled with shock-absorbing cartilage, lubricating membranes, and sacs called bursas whose purpose is to reduce friction and cushion the area between bones and tendons. Any of these knee components can be injured, especially when the leg is or knee is hit hard.

The most common knee injury occurs when one of the major ligaments is sprained or torn. The most often damaged ligament is the medial collateral ligament (MCL). This ligament can be sprained by a blow to the outside of the knee, especially when the foot is planted on the ice when the hit occurs. The blow causes the knee to move unnaturally and places strain on the ligament, often resulting in a tear. The treatment of choice for this injury is rest, compression, and ice.

A more serious injury is a tear in the anterior cruciate ligament (ACL). This kind of injury occurs when the hit is more severe or if the hockey player's knee rotates too much. If this ligament is torn, the player will often hear a loud pop followed by severe pain and an inability to stand or place weight on the leg. The loud pop is caused by the actual tearing of the ligament, which is tight and taut like a stretched rubber band. When it tears, the action is similar to the snap of a rubber band and produces a loud pop.

A torn ACL can be a career-ending injury, usually requiring surgery to repair the torn ligament. The ACL is the main stabilizer of the knee and is crucial to proper knee and leg function. An injury to this important ligament is often accompanied by injury to other ligaments and muscles in the knee, thus making recovery and repair of the injury much more difficult. Surgery is followed by five to six months of rehabilitation to strengthen the knee. Players often are required to wear a knee brace for several months when they return to the ice.

Concussions

While the use of helmets has decreased the incidence of concussions, this potentially severe injury to the brain is not uncommon in ice hockey. Helmets, however, do not prevent the kinds of whiplash injuries that can shake the brain back and forth within the skull, causing a concussion.

According to Allan M. Levy and Mark L. Fuerst, authors of *Sports Injury Handbook*, "a concussion is any loss of consciousness, even for a moment, or disorientation after a blow to the head."[40] Mangi, Jokl, and Dayton explain:

> A concussion literally means violent shaking of the brain. A blow to the head causes rapid acceleration and deceleration of the brain as it smacks against the skull on the side opposite to the blow. The brain and meninges [the lining of the brain] are injured, with bleeding into the brain and death of individual brain cells. There is a

A player with a concussion is removed from the ice on a stretcher. Collisions are the cause of many concussions in hockey.

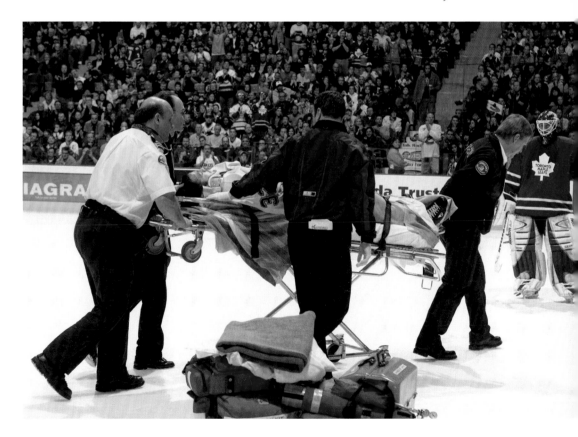

temporary disruption of the brain's normal functions, a scrambling of circuits, and a transient impairment of mental function.[41]

Most concussions occur because of collisions, either with another player or the boards. Levy and Fuerst write, "Hockey is a high-speed, high-impact sport. The bigger you are and the faster you go, the greater the impact from something or somebody hitting you. Although hockey players are not as big as football players, they travel at high speeds while gliding on ice and therefore experience much greater impacts."[42]

Physicians generally grade concussions on a scale of one to three, with three being the most serious. A player may be unconscious for several minutes from a grade 3 concussion. Individuals with a grade 3 concussion usually suffer severe confusion and dizziness. Recovery is slow. If a player is knocked out, he is kept immobile and a neck brace is placed on him to prevent the possibility of neck injury. "Any player who losses consciousness," write Mangi, Jokl, and Dayton, "should be sent to the hospital for evaluation."[43]

Occasionally a hard blow to the head can also fracture the bones of the skull. These fractures, which are typically depressed, causing the bones to press into the brain, can put pressure on the brain or tear blood vessels. This is a serious injury which can lead to a comatose state or even death. As a result, any blow to the head is treated as potentially life threatening.

A player who suffers a grade 1 or 2 concussion may merely be stunned for a few seconds and have trouble remembering where he is or what he is doing. In this level of head injury, there is usually no loss of consciousness. Players may have brief confusion, some temporary memory loss, and mild dizziness. Recovery from this type of concussion is usually fairly quick. Players with mild concussions can usually return to play minutes later.

No concussion, however, should be treated lightly. Abraham explains, "Any concussion is cause for concern. Even the ringing sensation after a collision or blow to the head—what used to be called 'having your bell run'—should be taken seriously."[44] A ringing sensation, called tinnitus, following a head injury often indicates the possibility of internal injury to the brain.

The treatment for concussion is rest to give the brain time to heal. Players are evaluated by a neurologist, a doctor who specializes in the nervous system, and tested extensively for severity of injury. These tests may include a computed tomography (CT) scan of the brain or a magnetic resonance imaging (MRI) scan to determine the extent of any brain injury. Both tests utilize X-rays to visualize brain or other tissue. A CT scan provides a three-dimensional image of the brain. As the patient lies in the scanner, the X-ray machine moves across the patient, taking a slice-by-slice picture of the brain. An MRI utilizes similar technology but provides

Jiri Fischer

Each team in the National Hockey League has its own team of doctors and trainers that attends every game. Usually the medical team treats players for the common injuries that occur during games. During one game in November 2005, however, medical personnel rushed to save a player who was having a medical emergency off the ice.

Shortly after leaving the ice during the game, Detroit Red Wing player Jiri Fischer suffered a heart seizure and collapsed on the bench. Medical personnel responded immediately, beginning cardiopulmonary resuscitation; they also used an automated external defibrillator to restart Fischer's heart. A defibrillator is often used in cases of cardiac arrest to send an electrical shock to the heart to get the heart to respond and beat again. In Fischer's case, the defibrillator did the job and his heart responded. He regained consciousness six minutes after collapsing. He was sent by ambulance to the nearest hospital.

After undergoing testing, Fischer was released from the hospital. Before his collapse, Fischer knew he had a heart abnormality, but since he had passed a stress test, he had been allowed to play hockey. (During a stress test, a person exercises on a treadmill to test heart and lung function.) After his cardiac arrest, however, Fischer did not return to hockey. Physicians told Fischer that playing ice hockey again was not recommended, and Fischer decided to retire.

a greater contrast between the different tissues in body parts, thus creating a better and more detailed picture of the problem.

In the first few hours after a concussion, doctors watch injured players carefully for any signs of severe headache, nausea, vomiting, and further loss of consciousness. All of these symptoms can be signs of internal bleeding.

Players in the National Hockey League are not allowed to play again until all of their symptoms are gone. Sometimes this takes a few days, and sometimes it takes a few months. Some players suffer from postconcussion syndrome and experience headaches, fatigue, dizziness, and impaired concentration or memory. Players must pass an extensive neurological exam before returning to the ice. This exam includes checks on a player's reflexes, muscle strength, balance, and the pressure in the back of the eyes.

Catastrophic Injuries

Most injuries in ice hockey are not immediately life threatening. Occasionally, however, catastrophic injuries do occur. Richard Zednik, a member of the Florida Panthers ice hockey team, for example, was on the ice on February 10, 2008, playing the Buffalo Sabres in Buffalo, New York. One of his teammates tripped over the leg of an opposing player and slid into Zednik, cutting his neck with his skate blade. Zednik, despite the severe injury, had the instinct to grab his neck and immediately skate to his bench, leaving behind a trail of blood on the ice. Journalist Steve Milton writes,

> With nine minutes and 56 seconds left in an intensely played game bearing serious playoff implications, Zednik drifted behind the Buffalo net and into a small scrum of players in the corner. Florida captain Olli Jokinen was upended and, as he fell, the razor sharp edge of his skate blade ran across the right side of Zednik's throat, slicing into the common carotid artery, the oxygen highway to the brain.[45]

An injury to the carotid artery is a catastrophic injury because the carotid artery is a large vessel that carries blood

and oxygen to the brain. Fortunately Zednik received immediate medical attention from Florida trainer Dave Zenobi and other medical personnel in the arena.

One of the medical professionals who responded was Les Bisson, an expert in catastrophic injuries. Using a rolled up towel to apply pressure to the injury, Bisson was able to control much of the bleeding until Zednik reached a hospital. From the time of the injury to Zednik's arrival at the hospital, only ten minutes passed. Bisson later stated, "This is one you hope would never happen. In a significant vascular injury scenario, the goal is to control it with pressure and get to an ambulance as quickly as humanly possible."[46]

Doctors reported that Zednik lost 5 pints (2,366ml) of blood. (The average human blood supply is 6 quarts, or 5.6 liters.) Doctors also noted that if the artery been completely severed, rather than just cut, Zednik could very well

Florida Panthers' Richard Zednik skates to the bench after having his throat cut by a player's skate in 2008. He lost five pints of blood.

have died. Physicians later credited Zednik's quick thinking and his determination to get to the bench as factors that helped save his life. In addition, medical personnel at the arena were praised for their quick and proper attention and treatment.

After a brief hospitalization, Zednik was released and placed on the team's injury list. He has since returned to professional hockey, now wearing a neck guard to prevent similar injuries. Efforts to require other hockey players to also wear neck guards in the National Hockey League have failed. Reporter Sarah Larimer explains, "The National Hockey League has always had a macho culture. Goalies didn't regularly wear facemasks until the 1960s and helmets weren't mandated for incoming players until eleven years after Minnesota North Star Bill Masterton died from striking his head on the ice in 1968."[47]

Holt Barrington is another hockey player who suffered a catastrophic injury. Barrington, a high school sophomore defenseman, was playing in a junior-varsity game in January 1998 when he suffered a severe injury to his cervical spine that caused a fracture between the fifth and sixth vertebrae in his neck. The injury occurred when he slammed headfirst into the boards.

Richard Zednik shows off the scar from his injury. He now wears a neck guard to prevent similar injuries.

Even though he was conscious and alert, Barrington could not move his arms or legs and was carried off the ice on a stretcher, fully immobilized. His coach, Ed Loiselle, called it a freak accident. Abraham explains, "Classically, a neck injury occurs when a player is hit from behind, flies into the boards and hits the top of the helmet against the boards with the neck bent forward."[48]

Following surgery to stabilize the fracture, Barrington was transferred to a long-term rehabilitation hospital. Initially doctors were hopeful that the young man would regain some use of his arms and legs, but Barrington's rehabilitation was unsuccessful. Today he is a quadriplegic and active in crusading for handicapped accessibility.

Retaliation

Many catastrophic injuries are caused by fighting between players. According to the Sports Injury Clinic, "it is not uncommon in sports such as hockey for fighting to break out and foul play to be committed. Estimations have shown that up to one-third of injuries occur during behavior which is outside of the rules of the game."[49]

When a player is injured by an opposing player during the game, his teammates often feel the need to retaliate or "get even." Often there is retribution during the same game or in the next game played against the team and player who caused the injury. While coaches and players generally deny any allegations of retaliation, the fact remains that this occurs with alarming frequency in professional hockey.

Such an incident occurred between the Vancouver Canucks and the Colorado Avalanche in 2004. Steve Moore, a player for the Avalanche, checked Canucks player Markus Naslund in the head while Naslund was reaching for a puck. Naslund suffered a concussion and missed three games as a result of the play. No penalty was called on the play, although the Canucks heavily criticized officials for their inaction. Vancouver players indicated they would get even with Moore during a future game.

On March 8, 2004, during a rematch between the two teams, a number of fights broke out between the Canucks and the Avalanche players. Late in the game, the Canucks sent one of their toughest players, Todd Bertuzzi, onto the ice. After failing to entice Moore to fight him, Bertuzzi skated after Moore and punched him in the head and then fell on top of him, along with several other players from both teams. Moore's head was driven into the ice during the fall. The result was three fractured neck vertebrae and a severe concussion. Moore was knocked unconscious for over ten minutes and he was carried off the ice on a stretcher.

Bertuzzi was immediately suspended by the National Hockey League for the remainder of the season and for the playoffs. Moore was in a Denver hospital for months before being released. He had to wear a neck brace for over a year, and he did not recover sufficiently to allow him to return to hockey.

Unfortunately, this is not an isolated incident. Retaliation is a problem that the National Hockey League has been unable to completely stop. Stiff penalties and suspensions are handed out, but in the heat and intensity of a game, such hits occur.

Injuries Add Up

Injuries, severe or otherwise, add up. Hockey is a rough game and the body of a hockey player takes the brunt of the roughness. Howard J. Green, a professor at the University of Waterloo in Ontario, Canada, says, "Hockey is uniquely stressful … the heat and humidity of the protective gear, the high level of coordination required, the repeated demands made on the muscles with little rest and the astounding requirement that it's played while balancing on skate blades are all factors [in fatigue and injuries.]"[50]

Trainer Rick Burrill says, "Hitting the boards sounds good in the stands. The fans love it and they rationalize it by saying it isn't as bad as it looks. They're right. It's not as bad as it looks each time. But they all add up. After a while, you end up with some kind of degenerative, arthritic condition that keeps you from playing competitive hockey."[51]

Player Brendan Curley, for example, was forced to stop playing hockey at the age of twenty-five. In addition to a bad back, Curley had severe tendonitis in both knees; he had broken his foot, shoulder, and nearly every toe on both feet during his brief hockey career. He also lost three teeth and counts himself lucky that his injuries are not more severe. His doctor told him that his knees resemble those of a much older person. Curley is unable to jog, ride a bicycle, or walk for long periods of time.

Ice hockey takes an incredible toll on a player's body. Despite the many advances in equipment, the penalties for fighting, and players keeping themselves in excellent physical condition, injuries remain a common part of the game.

CHAPTER 5

Fitness and Training

There has always been an emphasis on fitness in professional sports, but the 1960s saw this emphasis increase substantially. "Fitness fever" began in those years as more and more people took up exercise, as well as amateur sports. This led to a growing area of study that focused on proper conditioning and preventing injuries. This is when the modern era of sports medicine truly began.

Professional athletes also began to take a personal interest in not only their health but also in how they could prevent injuries and increase their endurance. Because injuries are a part of every athlete's life, a better understanding of how their body works is essential. It is necessary for athletes to learn how exercise can improve the body's functioning and what steps they must take to achieve the highest level of health and fitness.

A Demanding Game

Ice hockey is one of the most demanding sports in terms of the toll it takes on a player's body. Exhaustion is always a problem due to the face-paced nature of the sport. Alain Haché, author of *The Physics of Hockey*, explains,

Hockey's energy drain is greater than other team sports …
with National Hockey League players skating at speeds

in excess of 25 miles per hour (40 km/hr). The legend-ary Bobby Hull, fastest of his time, was once clocked at 29.2 mph (47 km/hr) and after he had spent twenty-nine minutes on the ice during one game, sports scientists fig-ured he had skated a total of about eight miles (13 km). So it's not surprising that during sixty minutes of regula-tion time, a player can burn several hundred calories and lose up to ten pounds (4.5 kg).[52]

Because of these high demands, most hockey players stay on the ice for periods of only thirty to eighty seconds. Player Doug Bodger explains why the short periods are necessary: "I don't think you're breathing half the time. You're mostly exhaling, pushing and shoving, and concentrating so much you don't think about breathing at all. That's why we can only stay out there for a minute at a time. It's like holding your breath."[53]

On average, hockey players are on the ice between fif-teen and twenty minutes in an average sixty-minute game. During that time, they are skating at peak speeds and mak-ing aggressive body contact with other players. This kind

Two players on the Florida Panthers execute a line change, where one player goes on the ice precisely as another comes off the ice. Most players are on the ice for thirty to eighty seconds at a time.

of performance requires players to be in top physical shape. Endurance is an important factor. The goal is for a player to be able to perform at the same high level at the end of the game as at the beginning. To do this, a player must be in peak physical condition.

Much of this conditioning takes place in the off-season as players prepare to face a long and exhausting season. Eighty-two games are held each season, and those who make it to the Stanley Cup finals can play an additional twenty-eight games. The season begins in October and can last well into June.

To make it through long games and a long season, hockey players must stay in the best possible condition. Former National Hockey League player and coach Wayne Gretzky explains, "For a better conditioned athlete there is less chance of injury, and conditioning promotes career longevity. The player also becomes mentally stronger, after enduring the intense efforts required for conditioning."[54]

Muscles

A hockey player's strength, skill, and endurance depend on well-developed and healthy muscles. The human body has more than six hundred different muscles, each of which is responsible for a specific task. Some muscles work alone, but the majority work together in groups. The primary function of muscles is to provide motion, but muscles also protect vital organs from injury. Muscles are also responsible for certain metabolic actions that occur each day, such as the beating of the heart, the breathing of air, and the digestion of food.

There are three different kinds of muscles in every human body: smooth, cardiac, and skeletal. Smooth muscle can be found in the stomach and intestines, while cardiac muscle is heart muscle. Skeletal muscle is by far the most common. Skeletal muscles are attached to the bones and provide motion. They are called voluntary muscles, because they are controlled by the brain in a conscious process.

Muscles provide movement by contracting and then relaxing. Myosin and actin, two bands of protein, play major roles in the contraction of skeletal muscle. The brain, spinal cord, and nerves also help the muscles work. The nerves connect the brain and spinal cord to the various muscles with nerve fibers called neurons. These neurons form a network through which nerve impulses travel from one synapse or contact point to another by way of the release of various chemicals. To bend the knee for example, the brain sends a chemical message down the spinal cord and then through the nerve transmission lines into the muscles surrounding the knee. As a result of these transmissions, the knee then bends. In fact, a message along one nerve can affect as many as one hundred small muscles. The body's muscles act like a machine by using energy efficiently and producing muscle activity.

Muscles can perform a variety of tasks. There are straightening muscles, such as the biceps in the arm, that help the arm straighten after bending; to bend the arm, the other large muscle, the triceps is used. The triceps is a bending muscle. Other muscles are classified as flexors; these bring adjacent body parts together. Extensors then move them apart. Abductor muscles move the arm away from the body, while adductors move it back. Pronator muscles help turn a body part, such as turning the hand face up, while supinators turn body parts down. Finally rotator muscles, such as the hip and shoulder, help a body part rotate. Most muscles are arranged in pairs, with one doing the contracting and the other doing the relaxing.

The Support System

Each muscle is surrounded by a sheath of connective tissue that encloses, supports, and connects other body parts. One example of connective tissue is the tendon, a strong band of tissue that connects muscle to bone. Tendons are tough but elastic and can be strengthened by exercise. They are also one of the body parts most subject to stress and inflammation, especially in a high-energy sport like ice hockey.

Ligaments are thinner bands of fibrous tissue; these connect bones to joints. Ligaments are fairly flexible but also subject to injury when overused. The healing process for

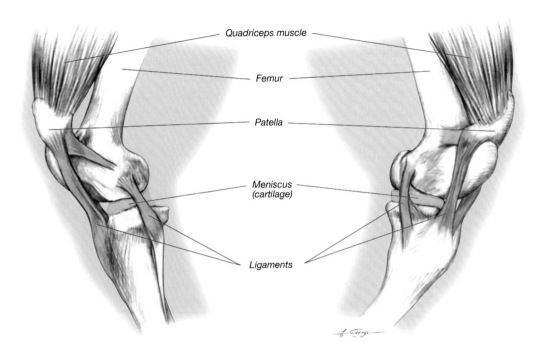

LATERAL   MEDIAL

Quadriceps muscle

Femur

Patella

Meniscus
(cartilage)

Ligaments

Ligaments connect bones and joints and are subject to injury when they are overused.

strained or torn ligaments and tendons is relatively slow as compared to the healing of a broken bone.

Joints are body parts that interact with the muscles to produce movement. Joints are composed of bone, cartilage, tendons, and ligaments. There are two kinds of joints: ball-and-socket joints, such as the hip and shoulder, and hinge joints, such as the knee and ankle.

Cartilage acts as a shock absorber for the body between the bones. Cartilage is composed of collagen, a protein also found in bone. Cartilage is primarily found at the ends of bones where the joints connect. Cartilage serves to keep the bones from moving against each other and causing pain.

Tendons have an inner sheath that contains fluid. This fluid acts as a lubricant so tendons can slide back and forth easily. When a tendon is overworked, the inner sheath can become inflamed and sore and may fill with extra fluid; this is called tendonitis. This condition is characterized by pain in the joint and surrounding tissue.

Muscular Activity and Energy

There is a complex process by which the body burns the fuel needed for energy and muscle contraction. In order for muscles to work at their optimum level, the body must consume various energy-giving foods, such as sugars and starches. When the food is digested, sugars and starches are converted into a substance called glycogen, or blood sugar, which is then stored in the liver and released as needed for energy.

Lactic Acid Buildup

Lactic acid is a by-product of exercise. During exercise, muscles convert glycogen (a form of glucose or sugar) to adenosine triphosphate (ATP). This is the necessary ingredient for muscles to contract. Muscle fibers convert various proteins and sugars into a compound called pyruvate. While some of this compound can be converted back to energy, most of it becomes lactic acid. Too much lactic acid can cause a muscle to become tired and stop working and can cause overall fatigue. Thus, lactic acid needs to be removed from the body following a heavy workout or a game.

The best way to do this is to continue to exercise but at a much slower pace. This is the reason many runners, after their races, continue to jog at a leisurely pace. Hockey players also do a variety of things to burn off excess lactic acid. Many ride a stationary bicycle while others do simple exercises in the locker room. A good massage also helps because it increases blood circulation and helps clean out built-up lactic acid in the muscles.

The following exercise demonstrates how the muscles tire from excess lactic acid:

Take an ordinary clothespin (the spring-loaded kind) and hold it between your thumb and index finger. Begin opening and closing the clothespin using only those fingers. After a minute of doing this, notice that you are slowing down. Count the times you are successful during the first minute and then compare it to the second minute. See if they are the same.

The Science of Hockey Web site states, "Odds are you slowed down significantly during your second minute [of the clothespin exercise].... You were exercising anaerobically, drawing on stores of glycogen to produce the ATP molecules that supply ... energy.... As the glycogen ran out, your muscles ran low on ATP and their ability to contract decreases."

Science of Hockey, "Fitness," Science of Hockey, www.exploratorium.edu/hockey/fitness.html.

During activity, the glycogen is broken down into lactic acid by the body; some of this lactic acid is then burned or combined with oxygen. During this process, carbon dioxide is formed, which in turn produces heat; muscles must be warm in order to work efficiently. A large majority of the carbon dioxide is then breathed out through the lungs, but a smaller amount is reconverted back to glycogen. This is a slow process.

Another body mechanism provides quick energy, namely the breakdown of phosphorus compounds in the muscle tissue. One of these compounds is adenosine triphosphate (ATP). This particular compound is responsible for quick energy and strong muscle contractions. If the body did not have this compound readily available, people could not participate in sports that require sudden bursts of energy.

How Does Exercise Work?

Ice hockey players, along with other athletes, must keep their muscles and support system working efficiently. Their bodies, therefore, need exercise. Exercise helps to strengthen the muscles and keeps a person fit to play strenuous sports, such as hockey. Scientists compare exercising to what happens when an automobile driver steps on the accelerator to make the car go. The fuel injectors feed more energy to the engine and, as a result, the engine goes faster. This process also occurs during exercise as the blood vessels carry oxygen and energy, in the form of glucose, to the muscles. In the article "How Exercise Works," author Craig Freudenrich writes, "In strenuous exercise, just about every system in your body either focuses its efforts on helping the muscles do their work, or it shuts down. For example, your heart beats faster … so that it can pump more blood to the muscles, and your stomach shuts down … so that it does not waste energy that the muscles can use."[55] Scientists have determined that a working muscle can take oxygen out of the blood three times more efficiently as your resting muscles. The more oxygen that reaches a muscle, the more effective and active that muscle can become.

The key organ in this process is the heart, a hollow pump made of muscle. Its function is to pump blood throughout the body. Blood travels from the heart to every organ and tissue in the body through a system of blood vessels. As blood passes through the right side of the heart, it is oxygenated or replenished with oxygen as it passes through the lungs. The blood is then pumped out to the rest of the body. About the size of a closed fist, the average person's heart beats about seventy times a minute. During high performance activities, like ice hockey, that rate can increase to more than twice normal, thus providing more oxygen to the muscles. During training, ice hockey players concentrate on improving their endurance on the ice. Thus an effort is made to increase cardiovascular output.

Kinds of Exercise

The body has two energy systems that are used during exercise or activity: the anaerobic system and the aerobic system. The anaerobic system does not require oxygen; the word *anaerobic* means "without oxygen." Fitness experts Jen Mueller and Nicole Nichols explain, "Anaerobic exercise is short-lasting, high-intensity activity, where your body's demand for oxygen exceeds the oxygen supply available. Anaerobic exercise relies on energy systems that are stored in the muscles … and is not dependent on oxygen."[56] This kind of exercise utilizes the high-energy stores of chemicals, such as ATP, that are necessary for muscle contraction. This kind of exercise is crucial for the typical hockey player who tends to be on the ice for short periods of time, followed by several minutes of rest. These shifts tend to be anaerobic in nature. The Sports Fitness Advisor Web site explains that these shifts feature "short, intense bouts of high speed skating and aggressive body contact, demanding a high level of anaerobic endurance."[57] Weight lifting is one example of anaerobic exercise.

For more intense exercise or activity, the body utilizes the aerobic system, a system that relies on oxygen for energy. The purpose of aerobic training is to push the body to extend its capabilities, especially cardiovascular and respiratory output. Hockey players, in particular,

Hockey player Manny Malhotra (pictured) does pull-ups to demonstrate the crucial need for anaerobic exercise in a hockey player's routine.

need increased aerobic capacity to perform; it is essential that enough oxygen is available to the muscles and tissues throughout a hockey game. Aerobic endurance helps players recover between shifts so that they can perform at the same level throughout the game. Swimming, running, and other active sports are considered aerobic.

Professional athletes use both of these forms of exercise to keep themselves in shape during the season as well as the off-season.

Stretching for Hockey

It is important for athletes at all levels to warm up and stretch prior to action. In his book, *Kids' Hockey: The Parents' Guide*, Gary Abraham, a sports medicine specialist in youth hockey, writes, "Muscles that are well stretched are less prone to injury."

Abraham and other physicians recommend several different stretching exercises for hockey players. The most important are leg stretches. A groin stretch is accomplished by keeping the feet together and the back straight while pressing the knees toward the ground. The hamstring stretch involves reaching as far as possible toward the toes of the opposite foot, then repeating it on the other side. The calf stretch is done leaning against a wall with the head up and the back straight; one foot is keep close to wall then the other is slid as far out as possible without taking either foot off the ground.

The quadriceps muscle, the large muscle connecting the thigh to the hip, is also important to hockey players. To stretch this large muscle, an athlete should lie on their side with the head supported by the lower arm. Then, with the other arm, grasp the foot of the upper leg and pull gently toward the buttocks. The exercise is then repeated on the other side.

A hip stretch is accomplished from a squatting position; one knee is bent forward toward the chest, while the other leg is extended as far as possible behind the knee on the ground. Finally a torso stretch can be done to work the upper body and trunk of the body. A hockey stick (or other sports equipment, such as a golf club or baseball bat) is placed across the shoulders and then rotated left and right with the upper body. Hold each stretch for a few seconds to stretch the torso muscles.

Gary Abraham, *Kids' Hockey: The Parents' Guide*, Ontario, Canada: Firefly, 2000, p. 100.

Hockey Warm-Up and Drills

Prior to the beginning of any hockey game, players focus on warming up. Allan M. Levy and Mark L. Fuerst, authors of *Sports Injury Handbook*, write, "Warm-up means warming up muscle fibers…. The warmer muscle fibers get, the softer and more fluid they become. They are then able to stretch more easily and to contract more rapidly. The faster a muscle contracts, the stronger it is."[58]

Part of this warm-up includes exercising. This exercising usually begins with upper and lower body stretches. Spectators to hockey games often see the players on the ice stretching leg and hip muscles, as well as rotating their shoulders and necks. Stretching in this manner is important in helping to prevent torn muscles.

In addition to stretching, players also skate as fast as they can down the length of the rink. They also practice skating backward and making sharp turns in all directions. These turns are especially important since during a game players will need to turn right and left while skating forward and backward. This ability to change direction quickly and efficiently is called agility. These drills also improve a player's balance and coordination. Fitness experts believe that coordination and balance are as important as speed in a player's agility.

Players also practice these skills during practice sessions between games. During these sessions, players participate in various speed and skating drills. They are asked to line up along one end of the ice and then skate forward as fast as possible toward the other end. They will then stop quickly and immediately sprint back to where they started. These bursts are done several times during practice. This kind of

Hockey players focus on warming up prior to a game. The team warm-up generally begins with body stretches like the ones pictured.

aerobic exercise is crucial for conditioning the heart and lungs for the intense bursts of speed and energy that are required during an actual game.

The drills and warm-up exercises also hone a hockey player's skills. Richard Mangi, Peter Jokl, and O. William Dayton, authors of the book *Sports Fitness and Training*, write, "To be a good hockey player, you must master the following skating skills: jumping, falling, stopping, quick starting, skating backward, and pivoting."[59] To accomplish these skills requires natural ability and lots of practice. Skaters practice with and without their sticks. Using their sticks, hockey players also skate in circles, going as fast as possible with the puck.

The Off-Season

Most ice hockey players work extremely hard during the off-season to keep in good shape. Mangi, Jokl, and Dayton write, "Hockey players must train year-round to maintain baseline fitness so they'll be ready to get into shape for the hockey season."[60]

Hockey players are encouraged to stay active during the off-season. Many play soccer, run, or cycle to stay fit. The majority of players also continue their regular season conditioning routine by lifting weights, riding a stationary bicycle, and running. Most exercise experts believe that an effective ice hockey training plan for the off-season should include a combination of strength and muscle building, as well as anaerobic and aerobic exercise.

Strength training is an important component in off-season training programs. While hockey players lift weights and do other muscle-building activities, their primary concern is muscle strengthening. The Sports Fitness Advisor Web site explains, "A physiological analysis of any game … will confirm that most athletes require explosive power, muscular endurance, maximal strength or some combination of all three in order to excel."[61]

POWER PLAY

During intermissions, a player's gloves must be specially dried out because of intense sweating of the hands during the game.

Most ice hockey players, like Rick Nash (pictured), work hard during the off-season to keep in shape.

Dehydration

Off-season and other conditioning can only do so much in preparing a hockey player for the rigors of the long season. A player can be in the best possible shape and still face problems on the ice. One of those problems is dehydration.

As muscles become more active, more chemical energy is transferred into heat and energy. The increased circulation of blood to the skin, for instance, produces sweat, which helps keep the body cool. This water, called the water debt, must be replenished by drinking sufficient liquids to replace the chemicals lost. Dehydration can actually lead to injury. The Sports Injury Clinic Web site explains, "If you become dehydrated, then less blood will flow through muscles. The muscles will be more prone to injury."[62]

Hockey players can be seen drinking water and other nutritional drinks during their time off the ice during games; goaltenders keep a water bottle on top of the net to replace their fluid loss. It is important for all athletes, professional and amateur, to drink lots of water and other fluids during any exercise or exertion that produces perspiration.

Hockey players, despite playing on cold ice, sweat profusely. Their time on the ice is intense and characterized by fast skating and lots of action. Players often leave the ice with perspiration dripping down their faces. Journalists for the *Guelph Mercury* newspaper in Guelph, Ontario, Canada, report, "Fully one-third of players who took part in a University of Guelph study were significantly dehydrated while on the ice, actually sweating more than some athletes thanks to all that heavy equipment and high-intensity bursts of skating."[63] Further research found that the majority of athletes became severely dehydrated during a sixty-minute hockey game. Symptoms of dehydration include muscle cramps, weak and rapid heartbeat, shallow breathing, and nausea.

To prevent these symptoms, players sometimes take extreme measures to prevent dehydration. Some players, for instance, drink energy drinks and other fluids. During an overtime playoff game in 2002, the Detroit Red Wings "downed water, energy drinks, and Pedialyte, which was designed for sick children but is great for professional athletes because it has a lot of electrolytes [vitamins and minerals the body needs] and is absorbed quickly,"[64] reports sportswriter Nicolas J. Cotsonika. During really long games, some players receive fluids intravenously (pumped directly into the blood stream).

Nutrition

In addition to conditioning and hydration, proper nutrition is also part of the preparation for a long hockey season. Most athletes require a higher energy or caloric intake than the average person. Levy and Fuerst explain, "To support, training, performance and health, you should eat a balanced diet of low-fat, moderate-protein, high carbohydrate foods and beverages."[65] The diet should be accompanied by plenty of fluids.

The three basic sources of nutrients for the body are carbohydrates, fats, and proteins. Carbohydrates are made up of sugars, while fats contain a high number of calories for the production of energy. Proteins are made up of a long chain of amino acids that provide further energy. Most nutritionists believe that anyone can obtain the proper nutrients from a good diet without the need for protein, vitamin, or mineral supplements.

Some hockey players eat a high-carbohydrate diet two to three days before a game in a practice called carbohydrate loading. Simple carbohydrates are made up of sugars, such as that found in candy. While athletes avoid candy, they do ingest larger than usual amounts of complex carbohydrates like those found in breads and pastas. Consuming a high-carbohydrate

Sports Medicine

The field of sports medicine has grown since the latter half of the twentieth century. This is due to several factors, the most important of which is that more and more people are engaging in amateur athletics and weekend sports. Most specialists agree that untrained athletes are most likely to get hurt. In addition, professional athletes today compete on a higher level than in the past. Sports medicine professionals are in great demand because of both groups of athletes.

Sports medicine is not a new science. In fact, it was practiced over four thousand years ago in Egypt. In 1898, around the time of the renewal of the ancient Olympic Games, the first English textbook on sports medicine was published. The United States formed the American College of Sports Medicine in 1954. In the early twenty-first century, nearly every high school, university, and professional sports team had their own sports medicine physician.

Sports medicine physicians specialize in joint injuries, orthopedics (bones), or kinesiology for muscles and movement. Podiatrists treat injuries to the feet, and physical therapists use exercise and other healing techniques to help rehabilitate injured muscles and bones. Acupuncture, an ancient form of Chinese healing that uses needles inserted into key body parts, is also a form of sports medicine, as is chiropractic manipulation and realignment.

Many injured professional athletes are treated by a team of specialists to ensure that they are in the best possible physical condition when they return to the playing field or hockey arena. They are aided in their return by hundreds of thousands of dollars worth of equipment that is not available to the amateur.

diet has been found to improve endurance. Carbohydrates are also essential for the refueling of muscles, as are proteins.

Any meal on the day of a game must be consumed several hours in advance of taking the ice. The reason for this is that the stomach needs an adequate blood supply to digest food. During a game, the body's internal control system redirects the blood flow from the stomach to other parts of the body. If a game is particularly long, players will occasionally consume energy bars during breaks in the action to increase energy.

Calories, a measure of energy, are used to measure the energy content of foods as well as the energy used by the body to perform certain activities. Thus, nutritionists can advise that running a certain distance will burn off a certain number of calories. The average inactive person requires approximately seventeen hundred calories a day. Caloric intake must be increased to allow for any additional physical exercise. An endurance athlete or a professional athlete may require as many as six thousand calories a day.

Hockey players drink water and sports drinks, like Gatorade, to have the energy and hydration to finish a game.

Trainers

Hockey team trainers are responsible for keeping the players in peak condition. For most hockey players, the team trainer is the person they need the most when injured or facing a long rehabilitation after an injury. In addition, the trainer is responsible for taping various parts of a player's body before games in an effort to protect knees, ankles, and other body parts from extra wear and tear.

Most teams also have massage therapists available before, during, and after a game. These therapists rub aching muscles in an effort to keep players on the ice longer. Massage

Team trainer Garrett Timms helps player Jack Hillen off the ice. Trainers are the first ones on the ice to assess and treat a player's injury.

therapy, which not only relaxes the muscle, but also increases the oxygen flow to the area, is also an important part of the healing and rehabilitation process after injury.

Sports medicine doctors are called in when a more serious injury requires professional care. Only a physician can deal with the many ailments that are associated with long-term stress on muscles, joints, and bones. These physicians can perform surgery to repair an injury or may prescribe medication to relieve pain. Sports medicine professionals are crucial in getting an injured player back into action as soon as possible. With access to the best available treatment, a player benefits substantially and loses less ice time.

Good conditioning, a proper diet, and hydration can all improve a player's performance and health. Mangi, Jokl, and Dayton summarize: "Unquestionably, today's athletes are vastly superior to those of just a few decades ago. In part this can be explained by increased opportunity and better nutrition, but much of the improvement is the result of modern training techniques."[66]

Chapter 1: A Lightning Fast Game: The Story of Hockey

1. Society for International Hockey Research, "The Society for International Hockey Research."
2. Alisha Jeter, "New Course Puts Golf into Its Misty Past Sculpture of Indians Playing Shinny Will Remind Golfers of How Game Might Have Begun," *Rocky Mountain News*, July 15, 1997.
3. Gary Abraham, *Kids' Hockey: The Parents' Guide*. Ontario, Canada: Firefly, 2000, p. 15.
4. Douglas Hunter, *A Breed Apart: An Illustrated History of Goaltending*. Chicago: Benchmark, 1995, p. 18.
5. Andrea Kannapell, "Heading Slowly into the Ice Age; Women's Hockey Is Growing, If Not at Olympic Speed," *New York Times*, February 17, 1998, www.nytimes.com/1998/02/17/nyregion/heading-slowly-into-ice-age-women-s-hockey-growing-if-not-olympic-speed.html.
6. Abraham, *Kids' Hockey*, p. 17.
7. Abraham, *Kids' Hockey*, p. 17.

Chapter 2: Ice, Skates, and Collisions

8. Melissa Russell-Ausley, "How Ice Rinks Work," HowStuffWorks.com, April 1, 2000, http://entertainment.howstuffworks.com/ice-rink.htm.
9. Quoted in Russell-Ausley, "How Ice Rinks Work."
10. Science of Hockey, "The Ice," Science of Hockey (Web site), www.exploratorium.edu/hockey/ice1.html.
11. Quoted in Science of Hockey, "The Ice."
12. Kirsten Weir, "Hot Shots: Hockey Plays by the Rule of Physics," *Current Science*, December 12, 2008.
13. Weir, "Hot Shots."
14. Science of Hockey, "Skating," Science of Hockey, www.exploratorium.edu/hockey/skating1.html.
15. Quoted in Science of Hockey, "Skating."
16. Laura Stamm, "Good Skater or Great Skater?" *Laura Stamm.com*. March–April 2008, www.laurastamm.com/tips/March–April2008.pdf.
17. Laura Stamm, "Circle Physics and Speed in Crossovers," Laura Stamm Power Skating (Web site), November

2004, www.laurastamm.net/power-skating-crossovers.aspx.

18. Stamm, "Circle Physics and Speed in Crossovers."

Chapter 3: Flexibility, Speed, and Reaction Time: Controlling the Puck

19. Andrew Franz, "Why Hockey Pucks Are Frozen," Helium, www.helium.com/items/1334372-why-freeze-a-puck.

20. Hockey Stick Expert, "Hockey Stick Lie—Get Your Angles Right for Better Puck Control," Hockey Stick Expert (Web site), http://hockeystickexpert.com/hockey-stick-lie-better-puck-control.

21. Science of Hockey, "The Gear," Science of Hockey, www.exploratorium.edu/hockey/gear1.html.

22. Angus McLean, "The Effect of Shape on the Flexibility of a Hockey Stick," paper, The Physics of Hockey (Web site), November 16, 2008, www.thephysicsofhockey.com/documents/shape.pdf.

23. Hockey Stick Expert, "Hockey Stick Flex: Produce Better Shots with the Right Flex/Stiffness," Hockey Stick Expert, http://hockeystickexpert.com/hockey-stick-flex.

24. Science of Hockey, "Shooting the Puck," Science of Hockey, www.exploratorium.edu/hockey/shooting1.html.

25. Weir, "Hot Shots."

26. Weir, "Hot Shots."

27. Dan Peterson, "Scientists Reveal the Secret to Hockey's Wrist Shot," LiveScience (Web site), May 29, 2009, www.livescience.com/culture/090529-sports-hockey-shots.html.

28. Science of Hockey, "Making Saves," Science of Hockey, www.exploratorium.edu/hockey/save1.html.

29. Charles Q. Choi, "Key to Hockey Goalie Success Discovered," LiveScience, October 26, 2006, www.livescience.com/health/061026_hockey_goalie.html.

30. Quoi, "Key to Hockey Goalie Success Discovered."

Chapter 4: Safety Gear and Injuries: Protecting the Players

31. Sportsinjuryclinic.net, "Ice Hockey Injuries," Sportsinjuryclinic.net, www.sportsinjuryclinic.net/sports/ice_hockey.php.

32. Quoted in Jen Waters, "Safety in the Game: Advances in Gear for Hockey and Players," *Washington Times*, January 6, 2005.

33. Quoted in Waters, "Safety in the Game."

34. Quoted in Sarah Larimer, "Even After Richard Zednik's Frightening Injury, Don't Expect Neck Guards in the NHL," *AP Worldstream*, February 13, 2008.

35. Hunter, *A Breed Apart*, p. 8.

36. Waters, "Safely in the Game."

37. Abraham, *Kids' Hockey*, p. 93.

38. Hunter, *A Breed Apart*, p. 123.

39. Richard Mangi, Peter Jokl, and O. William Dayton, *Sports Fitness and Training*. New York: Pantheon, 1987, p. 299.

40. Allan M. Levy and Mark L. Fuerst, *Sports Injury Handbook: Professional Advice for Amateur Athletes.* New York: Wiley, 1993, p. 49.

41. Mangi, Jokl, and Dayton, *Sports Fitness and Training*, p. 238.

42. Levy and Fuerst, *Sports Injury Handbook*, p. 189.

43. Mangi, Jokl, and Dayton, *Sports Fitness and Training*, p. 238.

44. Abraham, *Kids' Hockey*, p. 106.

45. Steve Milton, "Blood on the Ice," *Hamilton (Ontario) Spectator*, February 16, 2008.

46. Quoted in Milton, "Blood on the Ice."

47. Larimer, "Even After Richard Zednik's Frightening Injury."

48. Abraham, *Kids' Hockey*, p. 106.

49. Sportsinjuryclinic.net, "Ice Hockey Injuries."

50. Quoted in Anthony R. Edwards, "Biomechanics Powers Ice Hockey Performance," *BioMechanics*, September 2004.

51. Quoted in Jim Ducibella, "Warriors of Ice: Why Do Hockey Players Put Their Bodies Through All the Punishment?" *Virginian Pilot (Norfolk, VA)*, March 29, 1996.

Chapter 5: Fitness and Training

52. Quoted in Bill Sones and Rich Sones, "Hockey Burns Up Energy," *Deseret News (Salt Lake City, UT)*, January 3, 2008.

53. Quoted in Science of Hockey, "Hockey Fitness."

54. Quoted in Sports Fitness Advisor, "Ice Hockey Training Session," Sports Fitness Advisor (Web site), www.sports-fitness-advisor.com/ice-hockey-training.html.

55. Craig Freudenrich, "How Exercise Works," HowStuffWorks.com, November 27, 2006, http://health.howstuffworks.com/sports-physiology.htm.

56. Jen Mueller and Nicole Nichols, "Reference Guide to Anaerobic Exercise," SparkPeople, www.sparkpeople.com/resource/fitness_articles.asp?id=1035.

57. Quoted in Sports Fitness Advisor, "Ice Hockey Training Session."

58. Levy and Fuerst, *Sports Injury Handbook*, p. 3.

59. Mangi, Jokl, and Dayton, *Sports Fitness and Training*, p. 303.

60. Mangi, Jokl, and Dayton, *Sports Fitness and Training*, p. 302.

61. Sports Fitness Advisor, "Strength Training Section," Sports Fitness Advisor, www.sports-fitness-advisor.com/strengthtraining.html.

62. Sportsinjuryclinic.net, "Ice Hockey Injuries."

63. *Guelph Mercury*, "Hockey Research All Sweat," *Guelph (Ontario) Mercury*, February 5, 2008.

64. Nicolas J. Cotsonika, *Red Wings Essential*. Chicago, IL: Triumph, 2006, p. 118.

65. Levy and Fuerst, *Sports Injury Handbook*, p. 21.

66. Mangi, Jokl, and Dayton, *Sports Fitness and Training*, p. 6.

agility: The ability to change directions quickly and efficiently.

centrifugal force: A force upon a body moving along a curved path that is directed outward.

centripetal force: A force upon a body moving along a curved path that is directed toward the center of the curvature and keeps the body moving along the path.

checking: A physical action taken by a hockey player to stop an opponent from advancing down the ice or scoring.

concussion: An injury to the brain due to a blow or a fall.

crossover: The passing of the outside skate over the toe of the inside skate.

friction: A force that resists the motion between two bodies or substances in contact with each other.

goalie: The player who guards the net and tries to stop an opposing player from scoring.

inertia: Inactivity or rest.

momentum: The motion of a body.

puck: A round piece of hard rubber that is used in scoring in ice hockey.

reaction time: The time it takes a person to react to an action taken by another.

shootout: A one-on-one competition in which a player tries to score on the opposing goalie that is used to determine the winner of tie games.

slap shot: A powerful hockey shot that can propel the puck forward at great speeds.

sports medicine: A field of study and practice focused on preventing and treating sports injuries.

velocity: The rate at which an object changes its position.

vulcanization: A chemical process for converting rubber into more durable materials through the use of high pressure and temperature.

weight transfer: The transfer of weight and energy when an object's center of gravity shifts.

Books

Edward Edelson, *Sports Medicine*. Philadelphia, PA: Chelsea House, 2000. An examination of body physiology and the stress of sports, along with nutrition and fitness.

Robert Gardner, *Experimenting with Science in Sports*. New York: Franklin Watts, 1993. A good book about the science behind sports, such as the velocity of hockey pucks and footwear and friction.

Robert Gardner, *Science Projects About the Physics of Sports*. Berkeley Heights, NJ: Enslow, 2000. This book contains a number of experiments related to the physics of hockey; specifically the concepts of speed, gravity, and momentum.

Michael McKinley, *Ice Time: The Story of Hockey*. Toronto, Canada: Tundra, 2006. A book that gives an overall look at hockey; its history; and its greatest players.

Internet Sources

Ed Grabianowski, "How Hockey Works," HowStuffWorks.com, June 5, 2003, http://entertainment.howstuffworks.com/hockey.htm.

How Products Are Made, "Hockey Stick," How Products Are Made, www.madehow.com/Volume-4/Hockey-Stick.html.

Science of Hockey, "The Gear," Science of Hockey, www.exploratorium.edu/hockey/gear1.html.

Periodicals

Associated Press, "Fischer Suffers Seizure on Red Wings Bench," *AP Online*, November 22, 2005.

David Elfin, "On Ice Safety is Secondary," *Insight on the News*, May 13, 2002.

Nina Wegner, "Out of the Class, Onto the Ice," *Post Standard (Syracuse, NY)*, February 26, 2009.

Videos

"How It's Made: Hockey Blades" Discovery Channel video, 2009. http://science.discovery.com/videos/how-its-made-hockey-blades.html.

"100 Greatest Discoveries: Laws of Motion" Science Channel video, 2009. http://science.discovery.com/videos/100-greatest-discoveries-shorts-laws-of-motion.html.

Web Sites

Canadian Hockey Association (www.canadianhockey.ca). This is Canada's governing body for hockey.

USA Hockey (www.usahockey.com). This group is the governing body for hockey in the United States.

National Hockey League (www.nhl.com). This site offers current statistics, player profiles, and other information about professional hockey.

INDEX

PICTURE CREDITS

Cover Photos: © 2010. Photos.com, a division of Getty Images; Jupiterimages/liquidlibrary/Thinkstock

© 19th era/Alamy, 34

© Ancient Art & Architecture Collection Ltd/Alamy, 7

Andy Devlin/NHLI via Getty Images, 69

AP Images, 17, 41, 63, 77, 78, 90, 92, 94, 97, 98

© Bettmann/Corbis, 11, 47, 67

Bruce Bennett Studios/Getty Images, 12

Bruce Bennett/Getty Images, 22, 35, 49

Dave Reginek/NHLI via Getty Images, 26, 53

© FocusEurope/Alamy, 32

Gale, Cengage Learning, 13, 30, 52, 54, 64, 71

Jarmila Kovarikova/isifa/Getty Images, 45

Jeff Vinnick/Getty Images/NHLI, 73

© Joe Fox/Alamy, 65

Joel Auerbach/Getty Images, 83

© Michael Ventura/Alamy, 28

Nick Didlick/Getty Images, 58

© Oliver Dixon/Alamy, 39

© PHOTOTAKE Inc./Alamy, 86

© PRISMA ARCHIVO/Alamy, 19

© RIA Novosti/Alamy, 57

© Stefan Sollfors/Alamy, 16

© Wally McNamee/Corbis, 20

© William Manning/Corbis, 37

ABOUT THE AUTHOR

Anne Wallace Sharp is the author of the adult book *Gifts*; several children's books, including *Daring Pirate Women*; and seventeen other Lucent Books. She has also written numerous magazine articles for both adults and juveniles. A retired registered nurse, Sharp has a degree in history. Her interests include reading, traveling, and spending time with her two grandchildren, Jacob and Nicole. She is also an avid ice hockey fan. Sharp lives in Beavercreek, Ohio.